This Book Belongs to:

....

MMG PUBLISHING

THANK YOU FOR PURCHASING THIS BOOK. IF YOU ENJOYED THIS TITLE, FEEDBACK ON AMAZON WOULD BE GREATLY APPRECIATED. IF YOU HAD ANY ISSUES, THEN PLEASE DROP US AN EMAIL VIA CLUNKABLE@GMAIL.COM

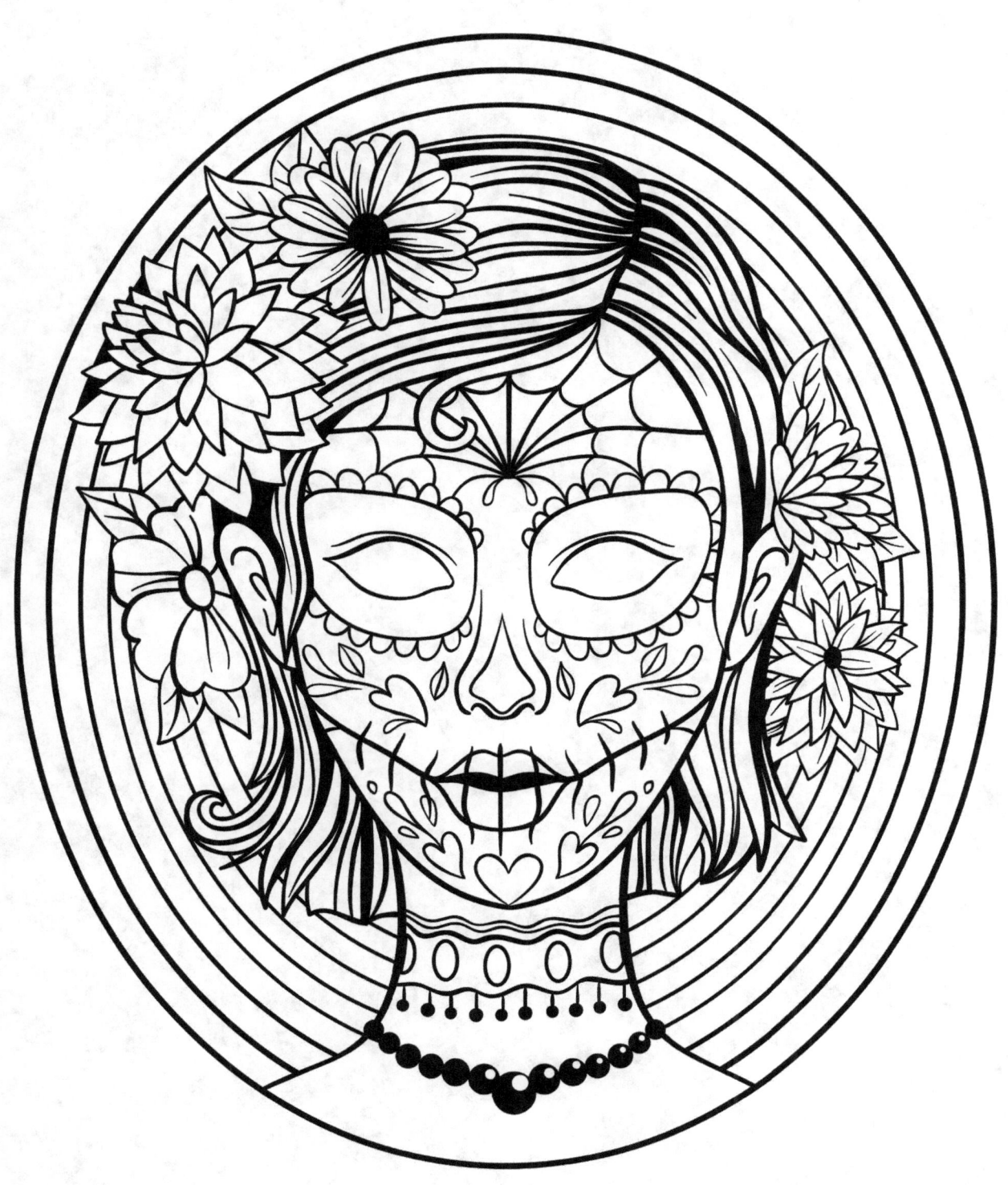

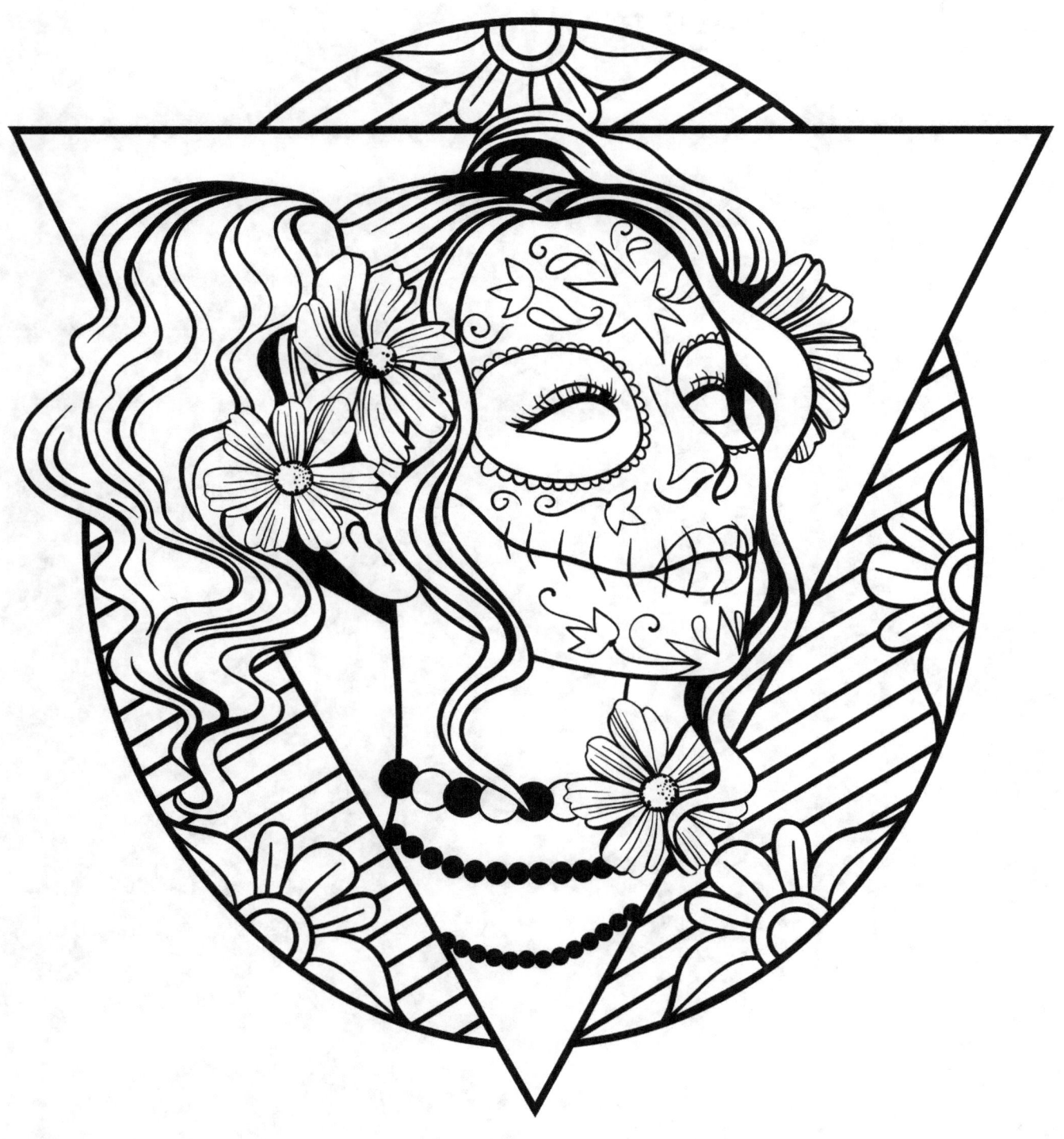

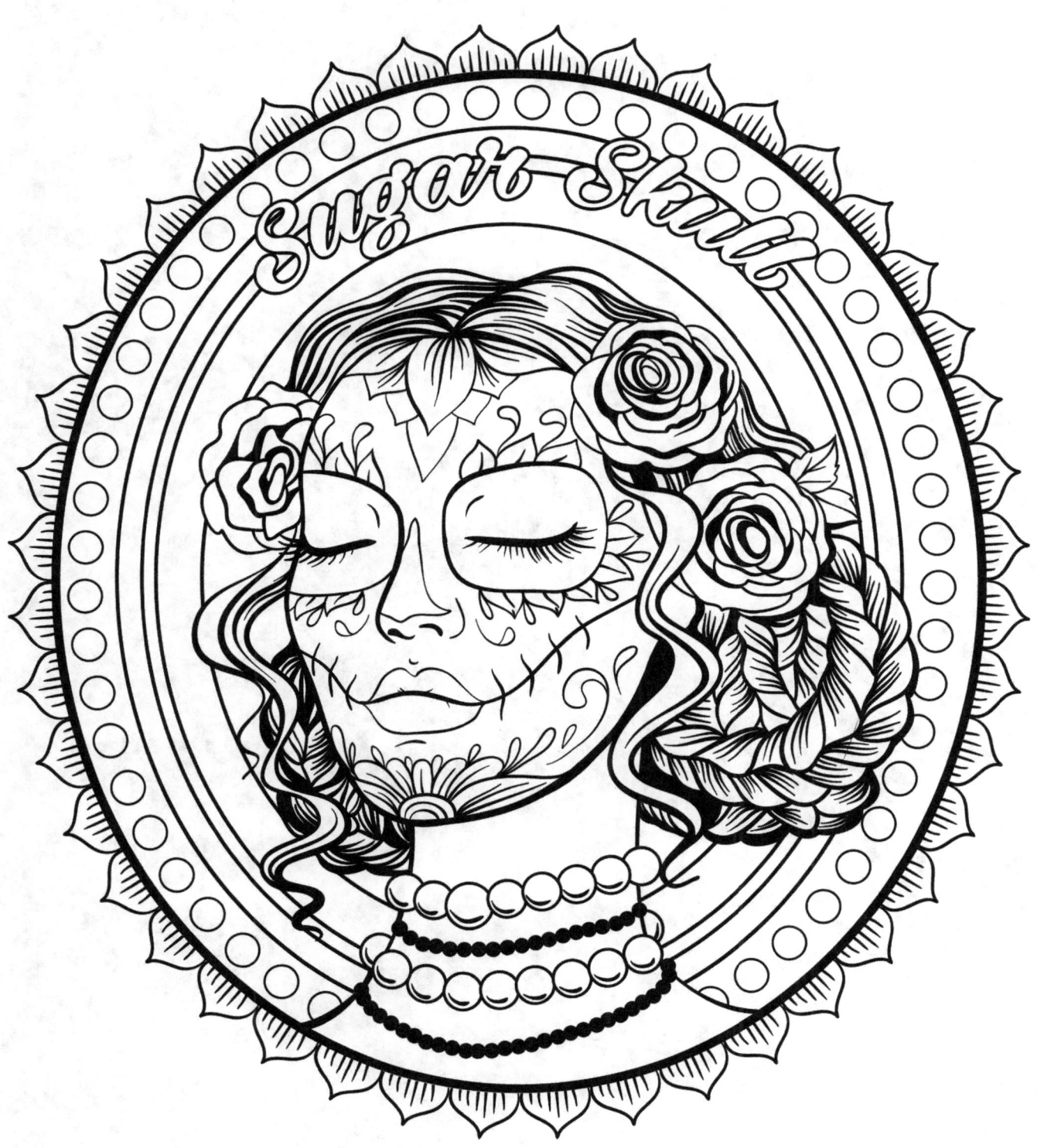

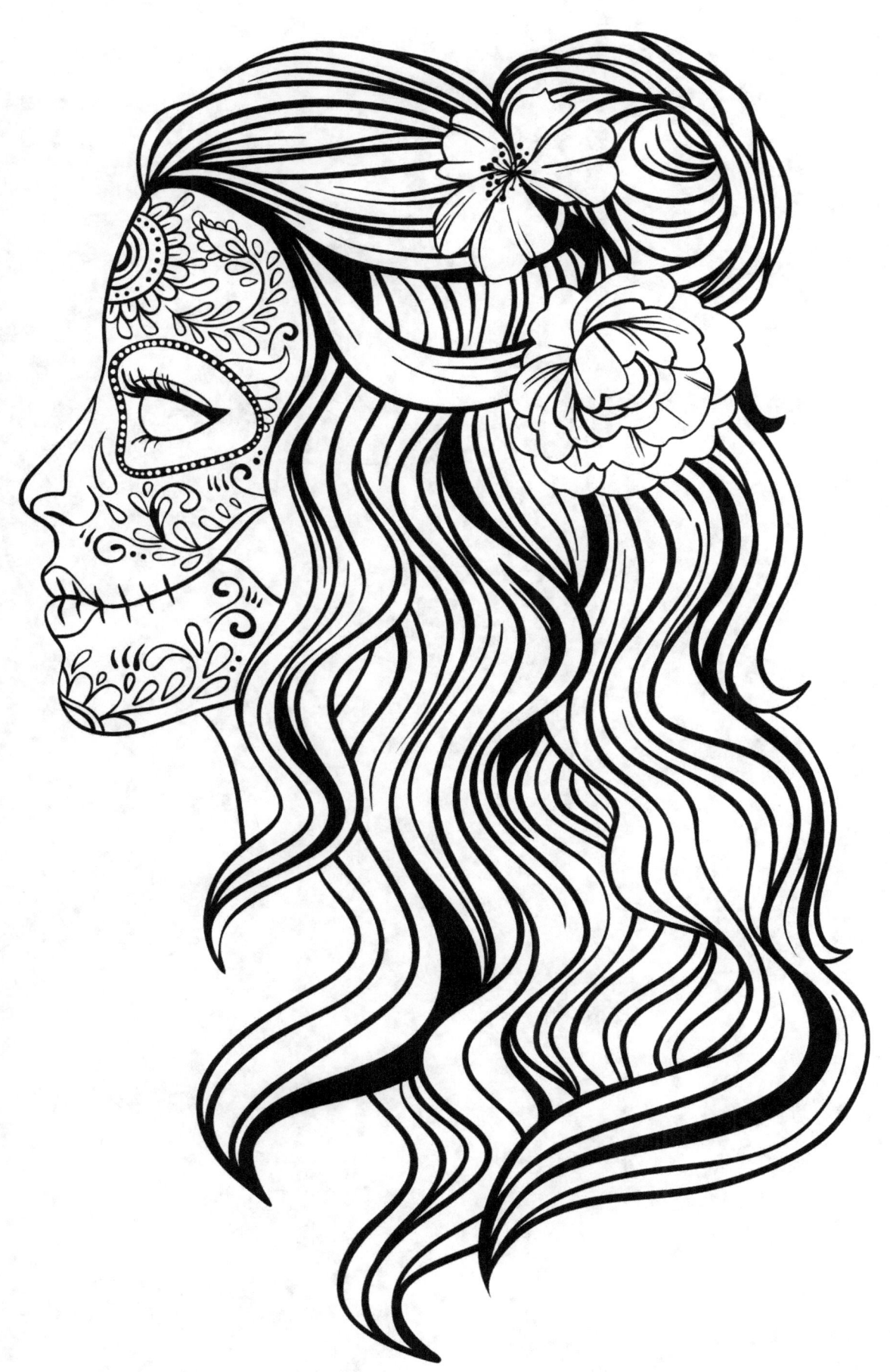

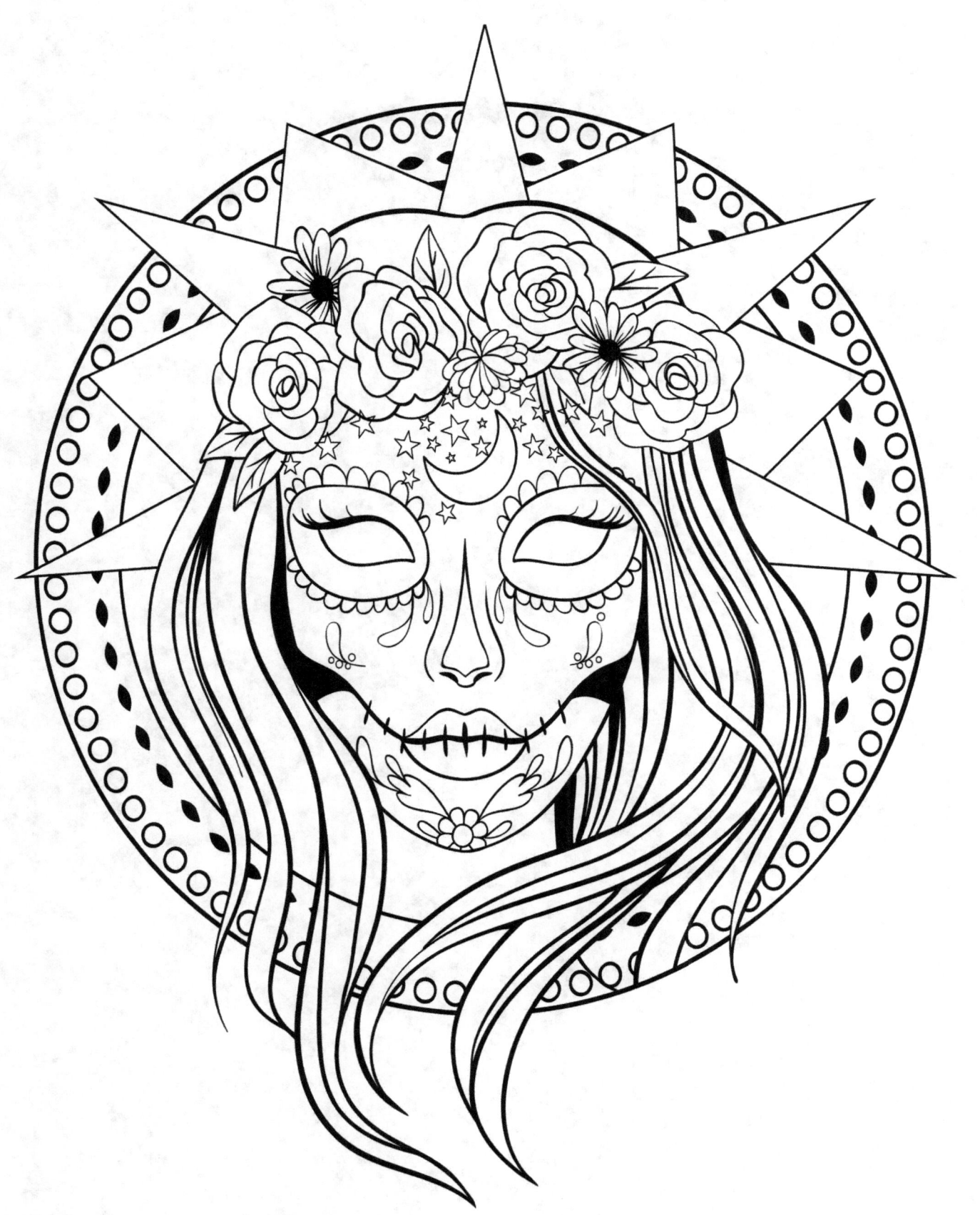

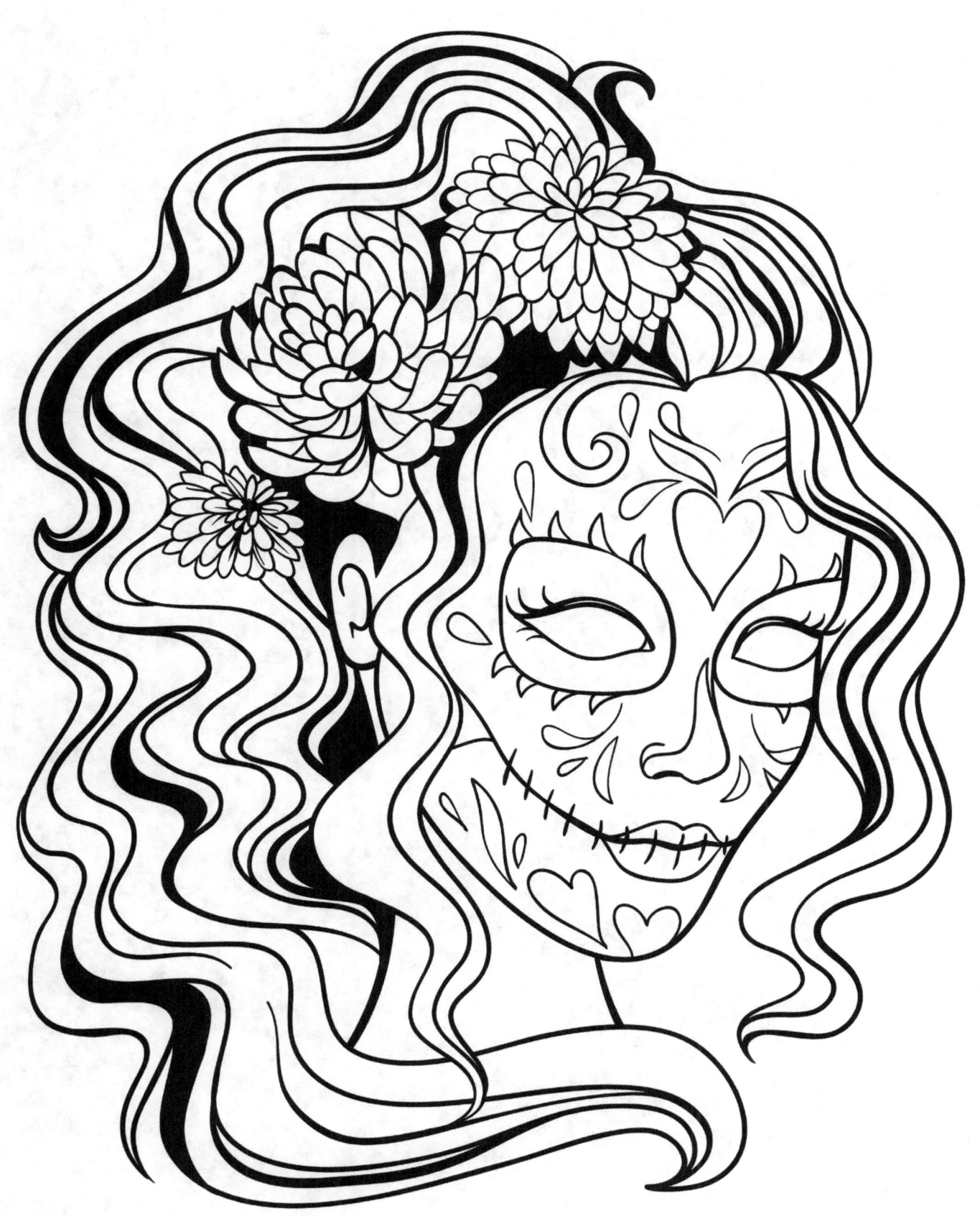

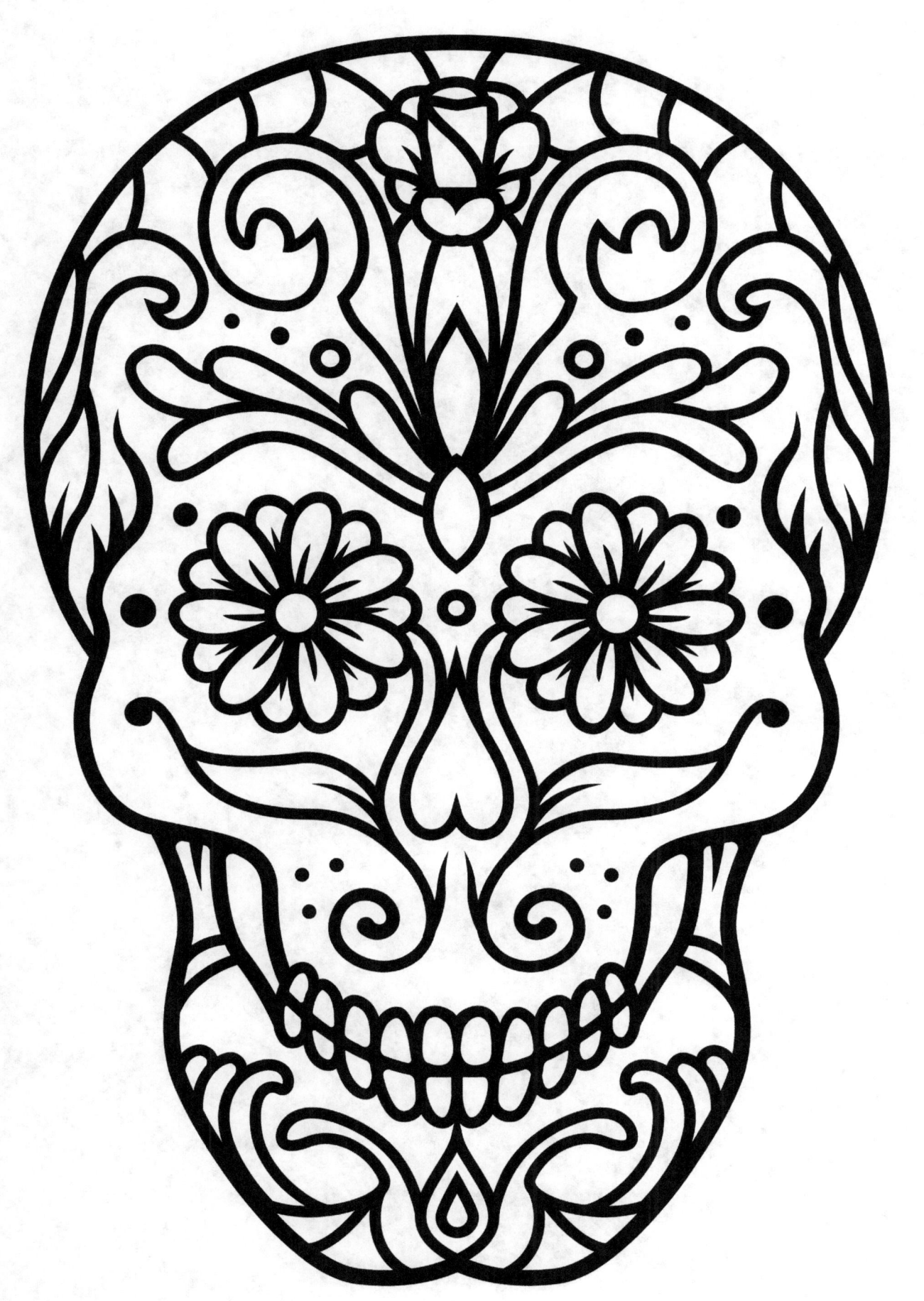

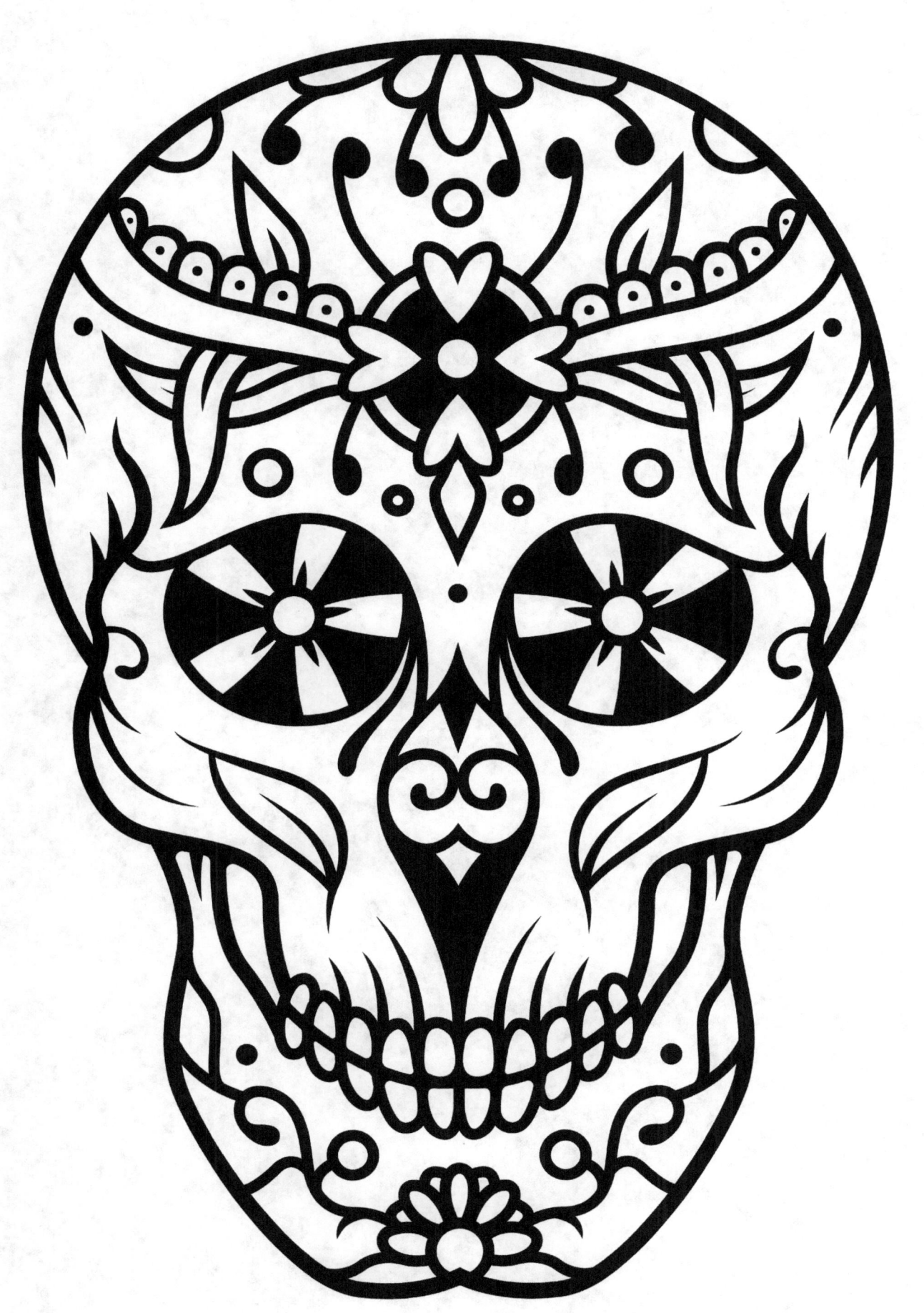

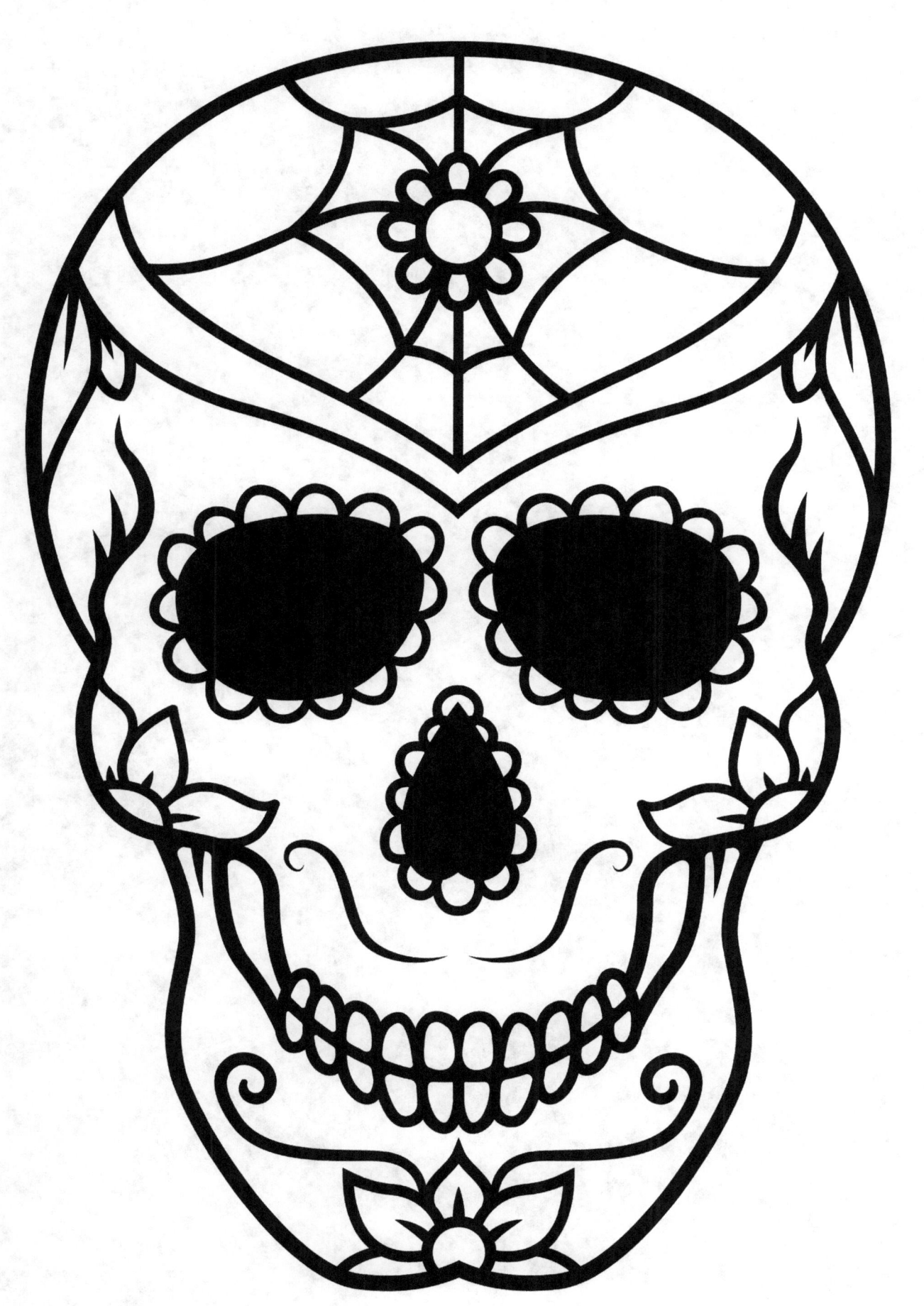

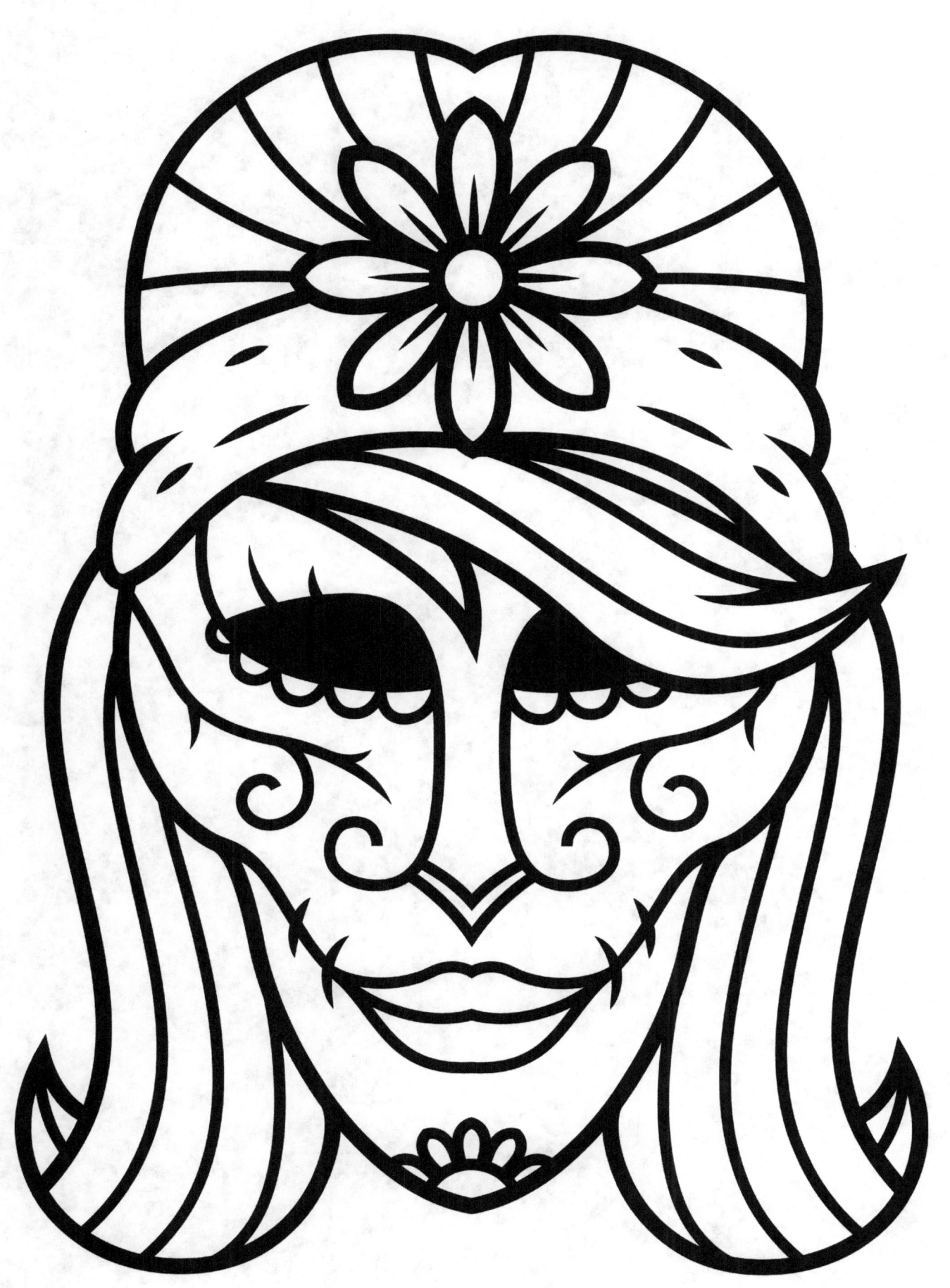

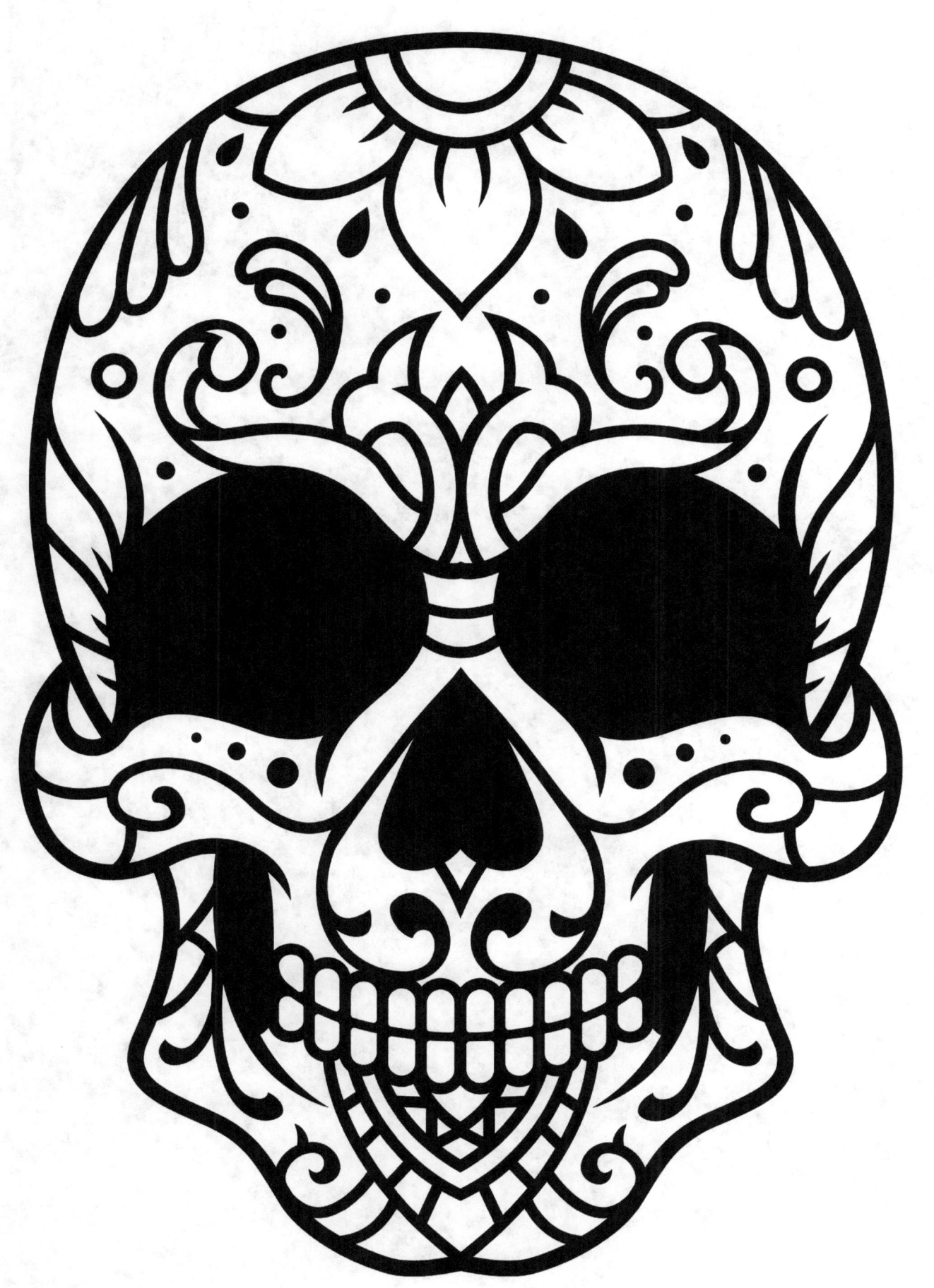

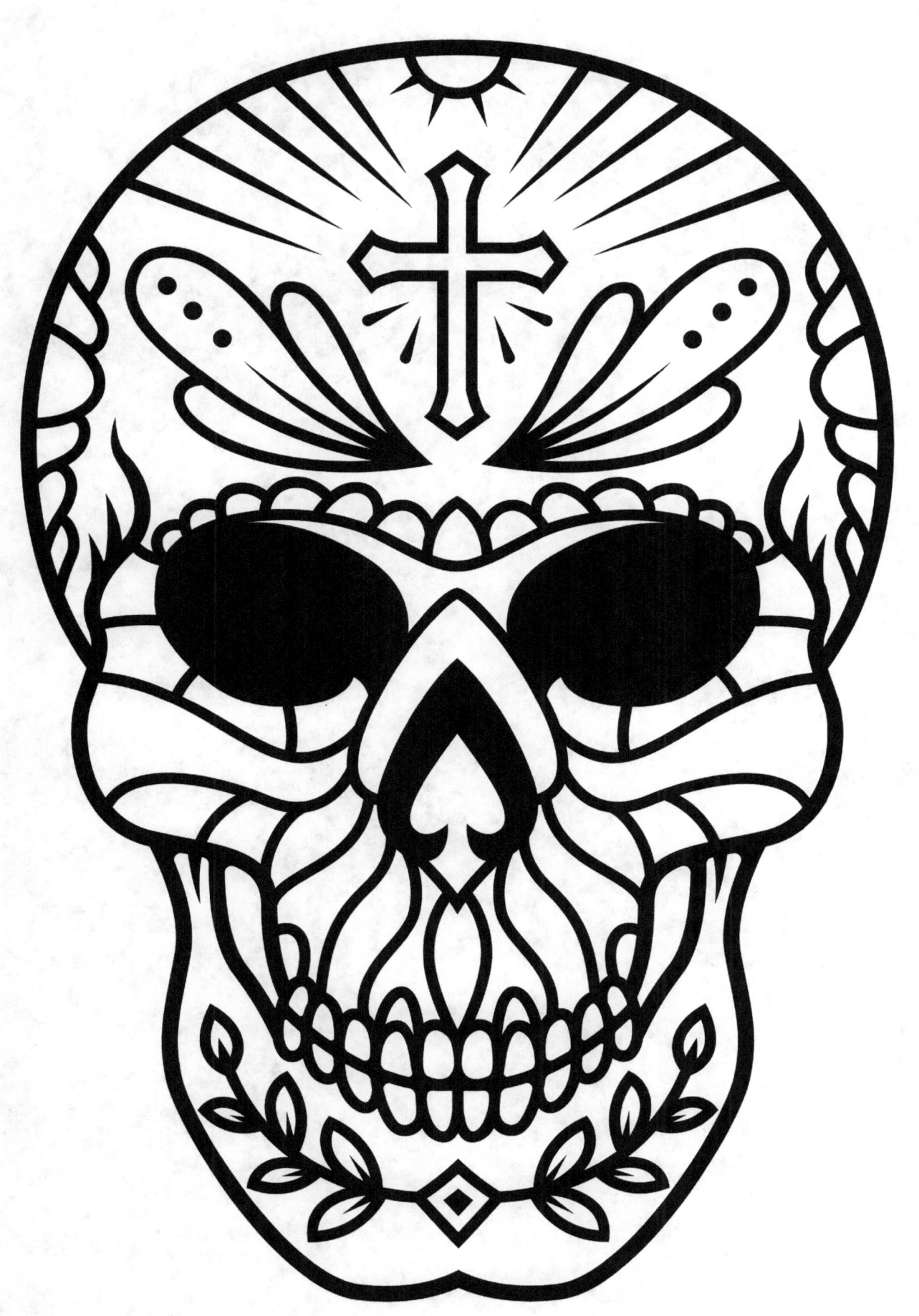

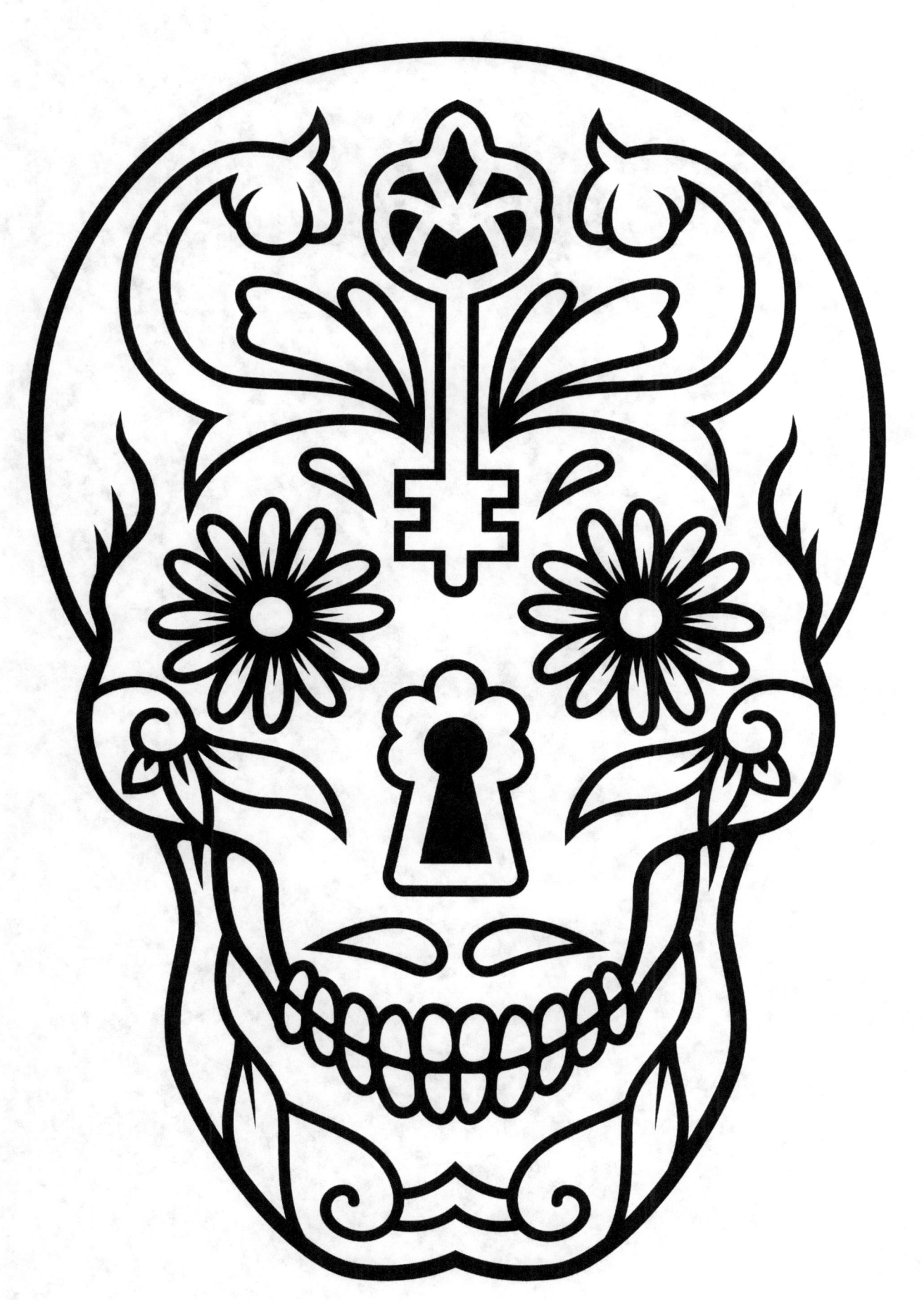

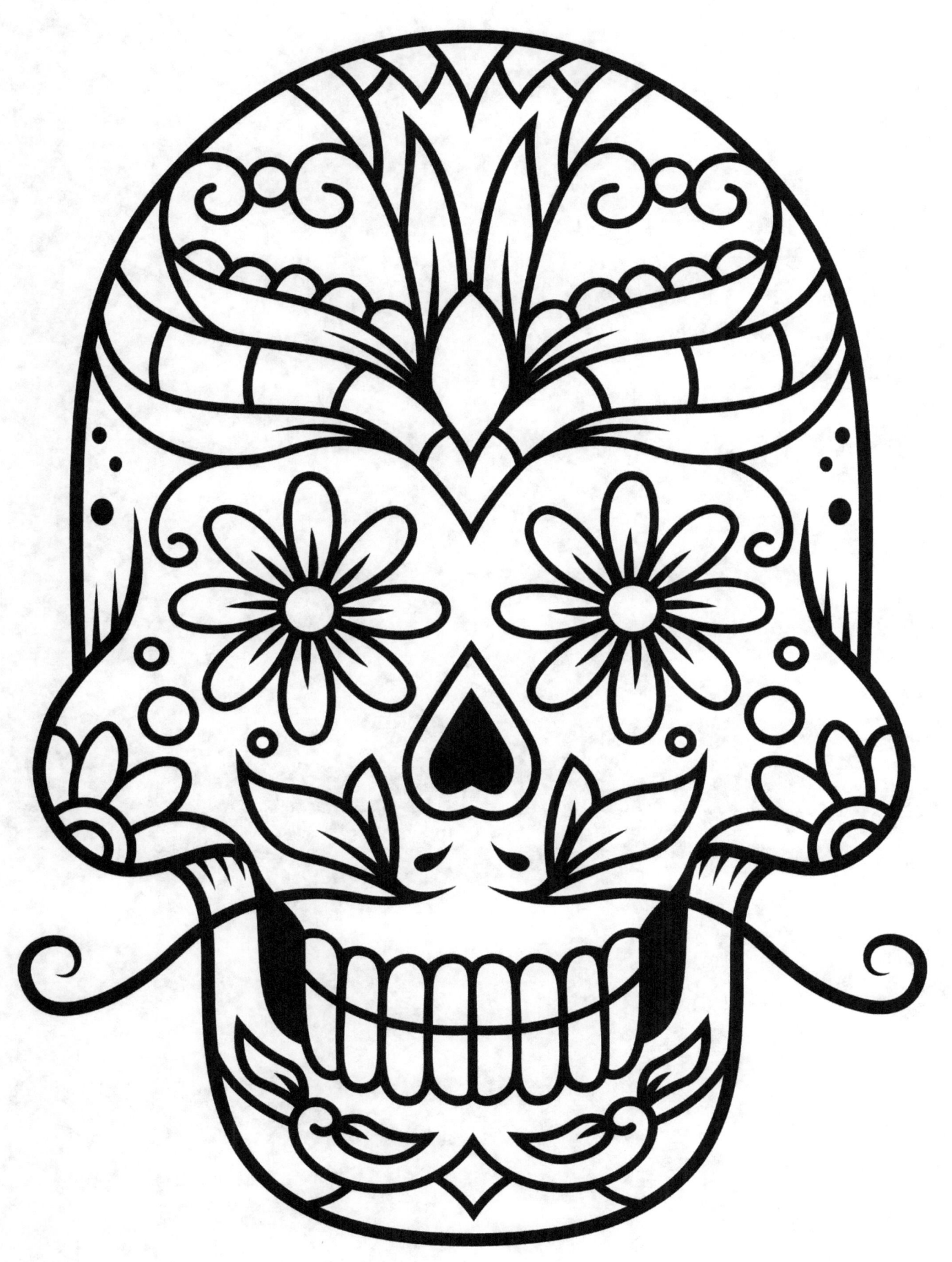

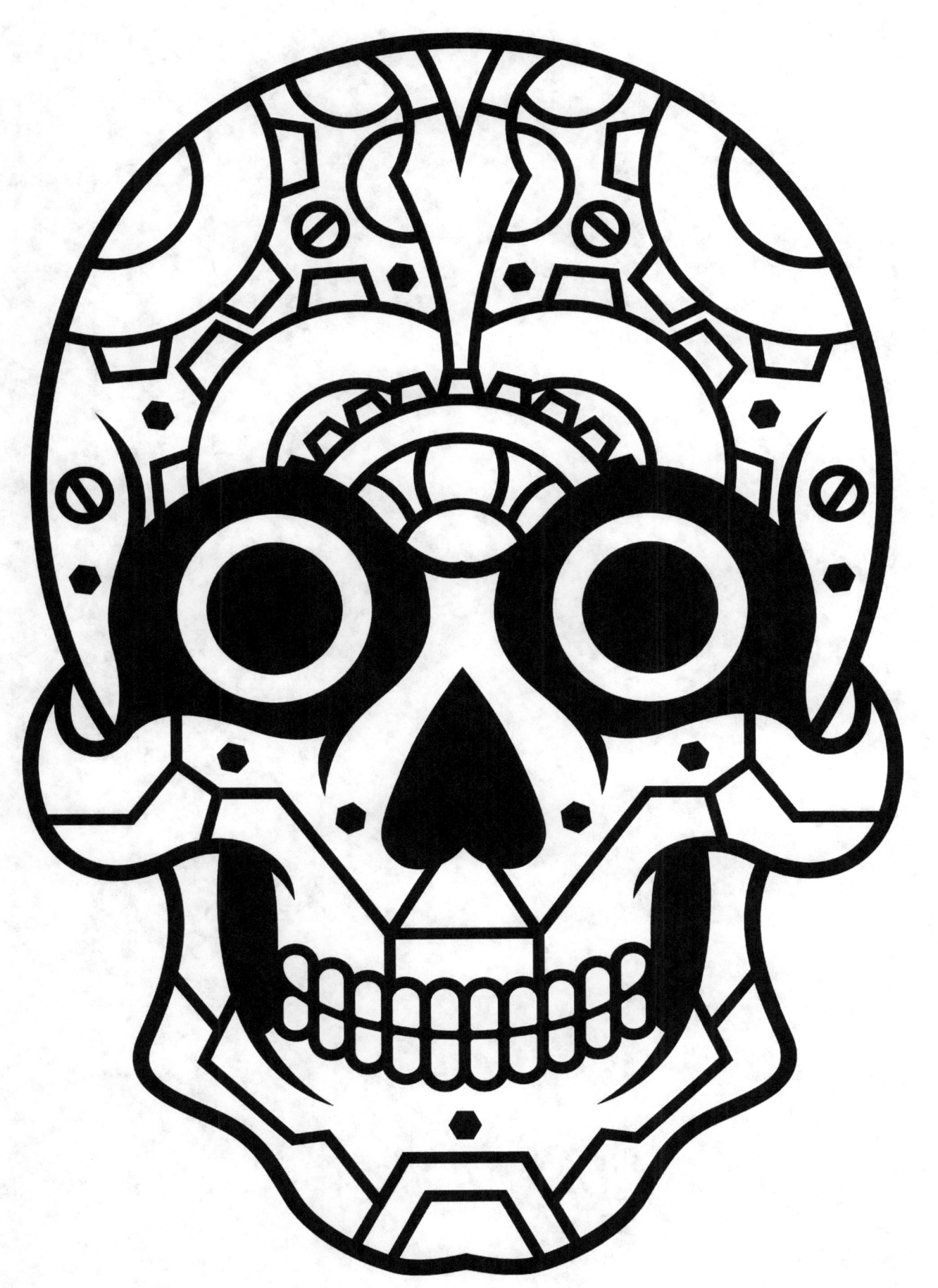

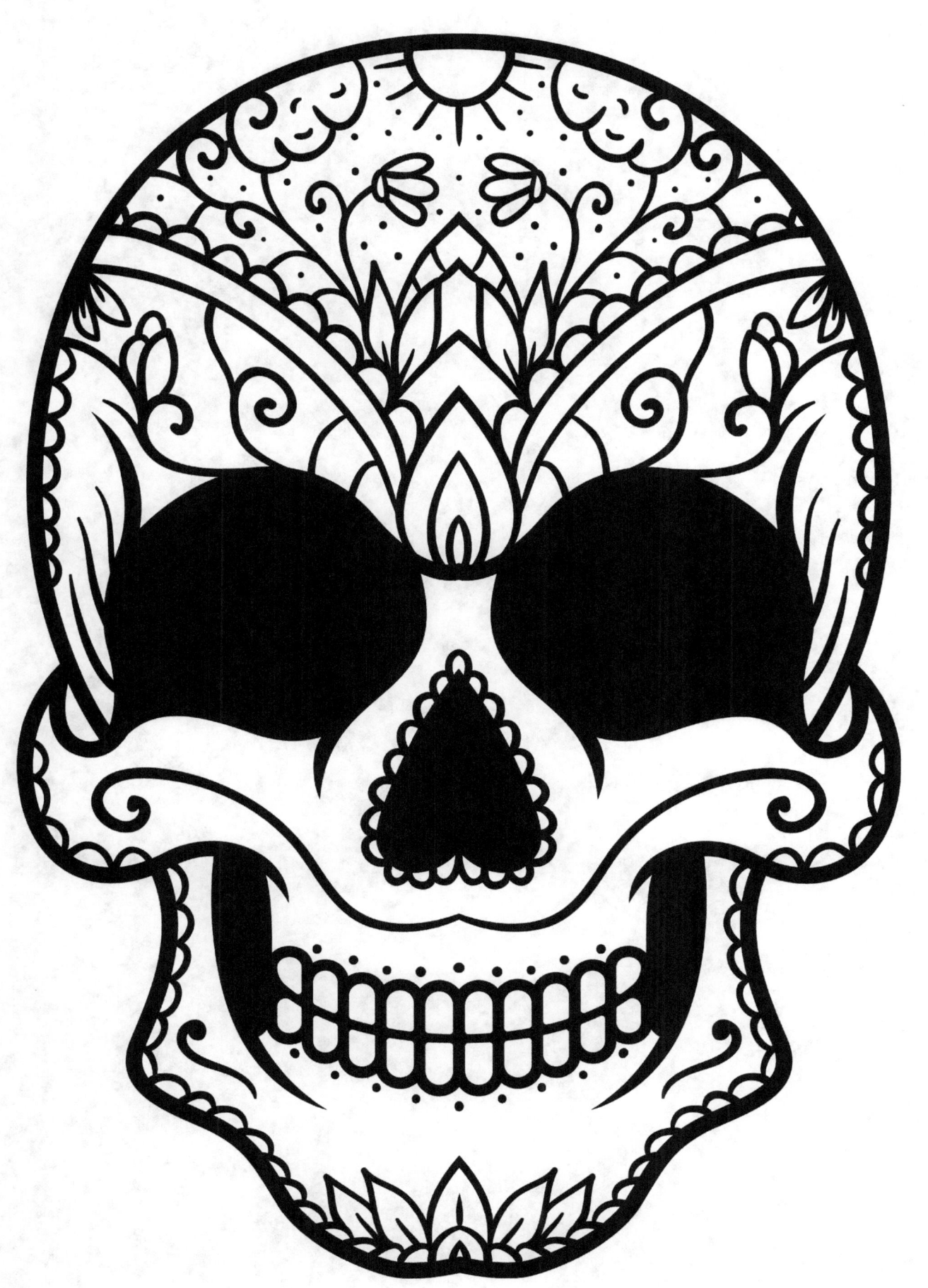

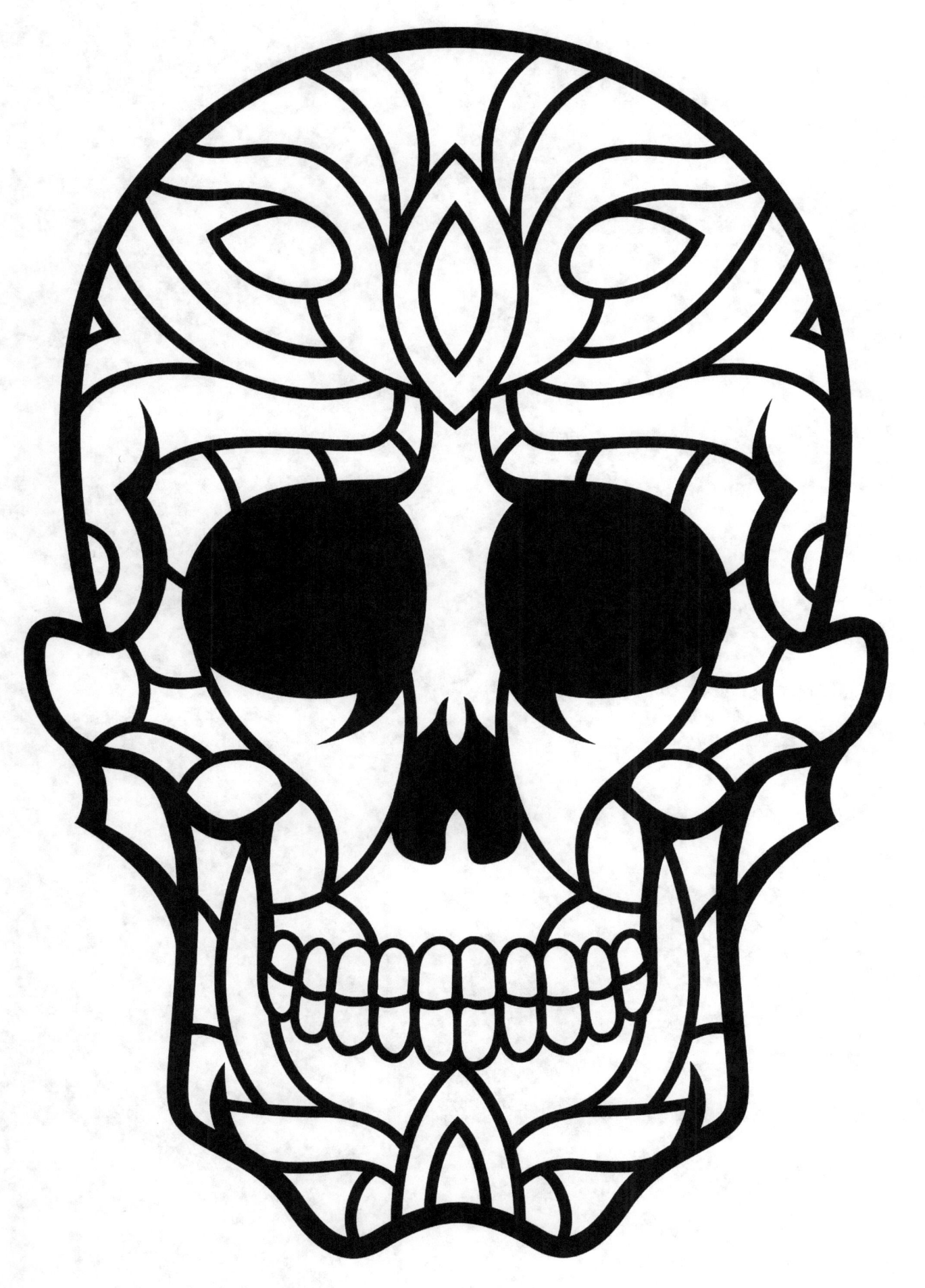

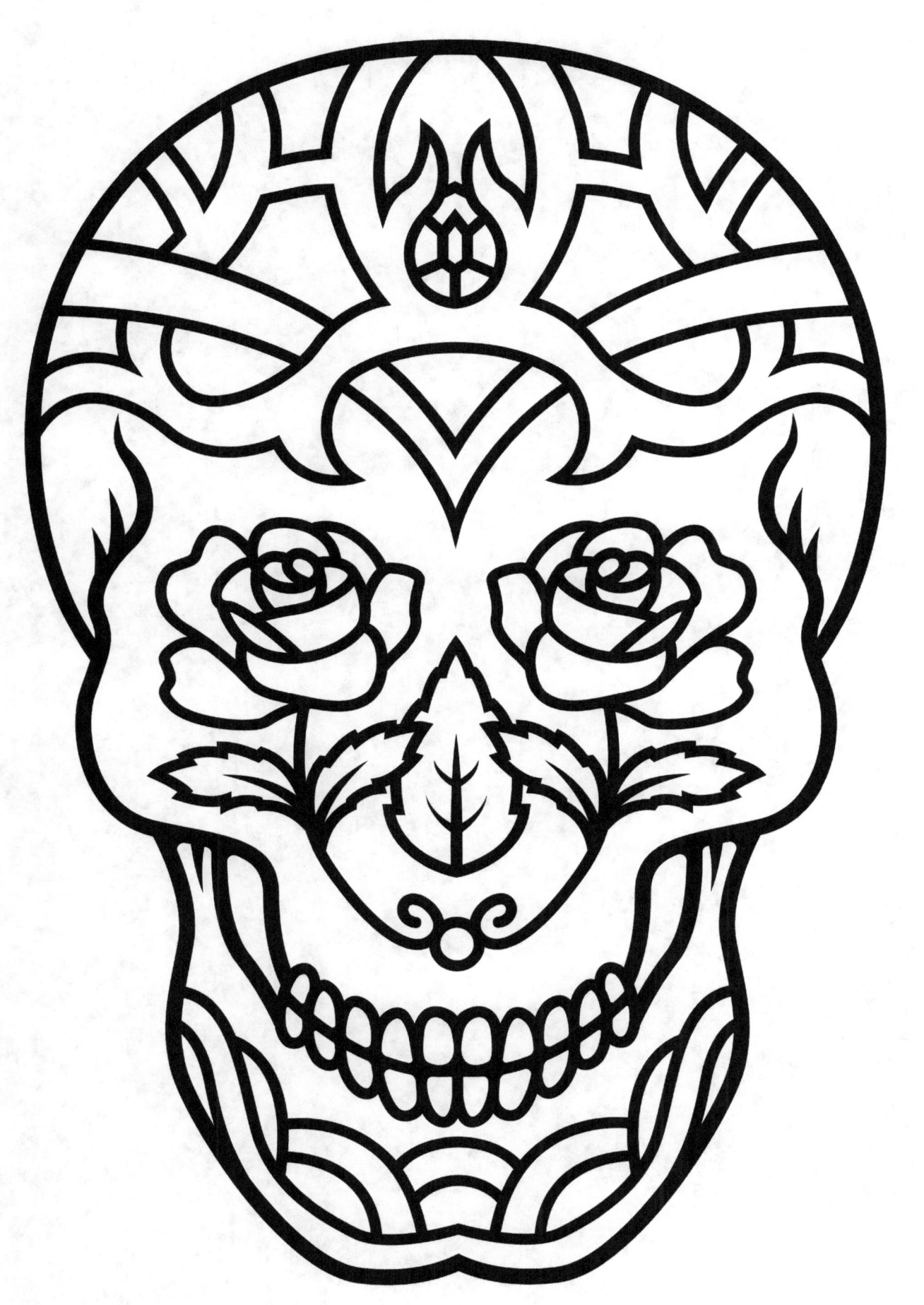

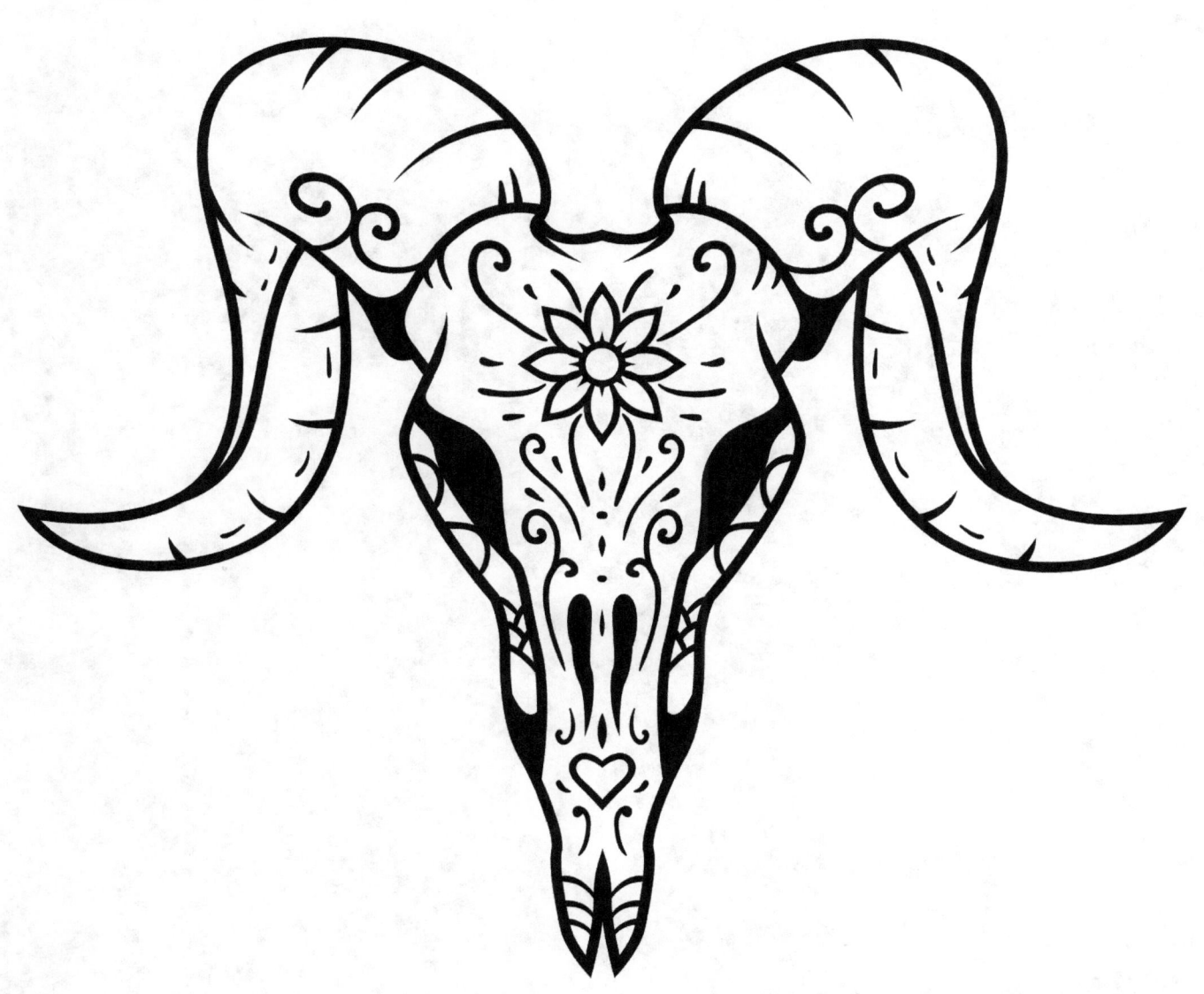

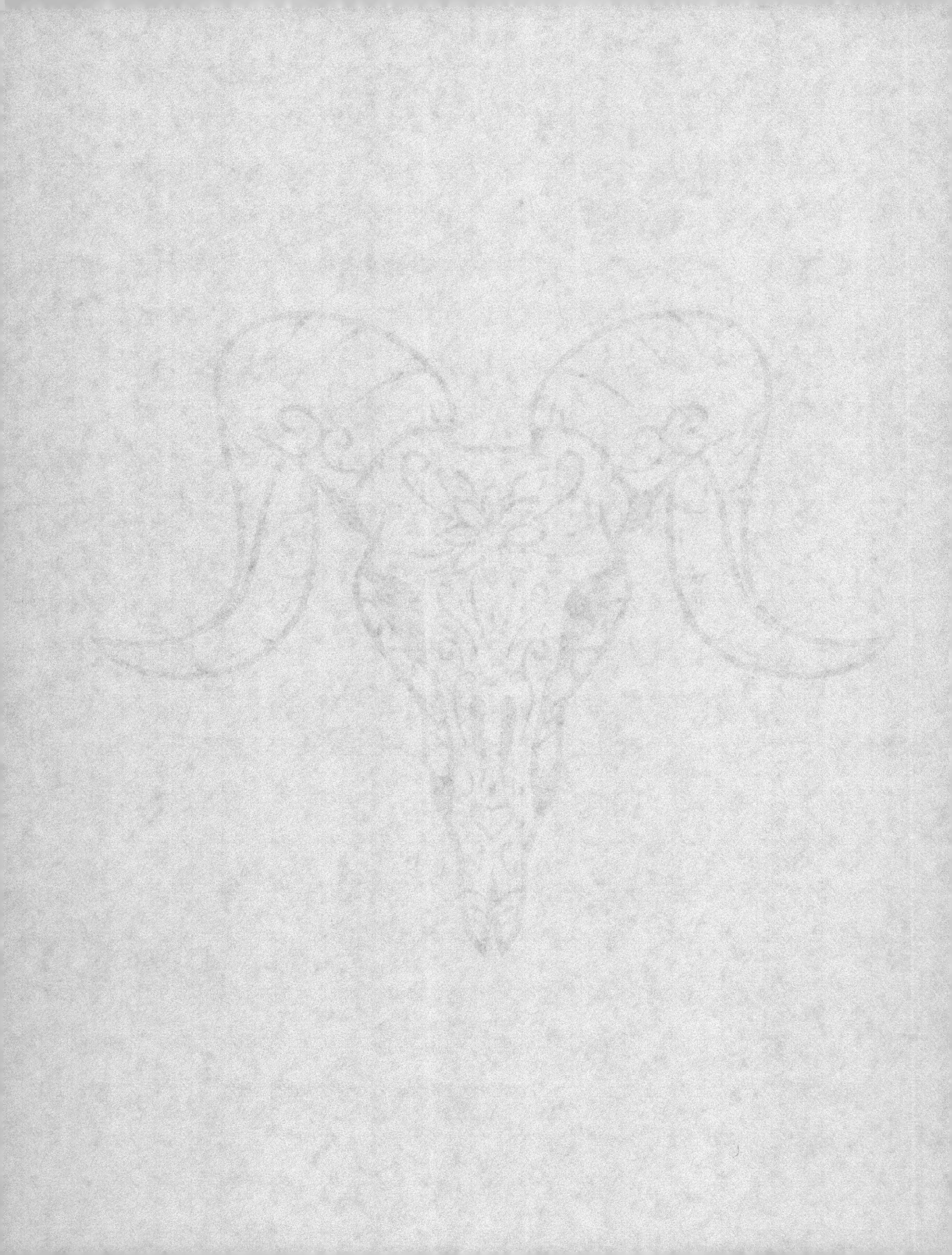

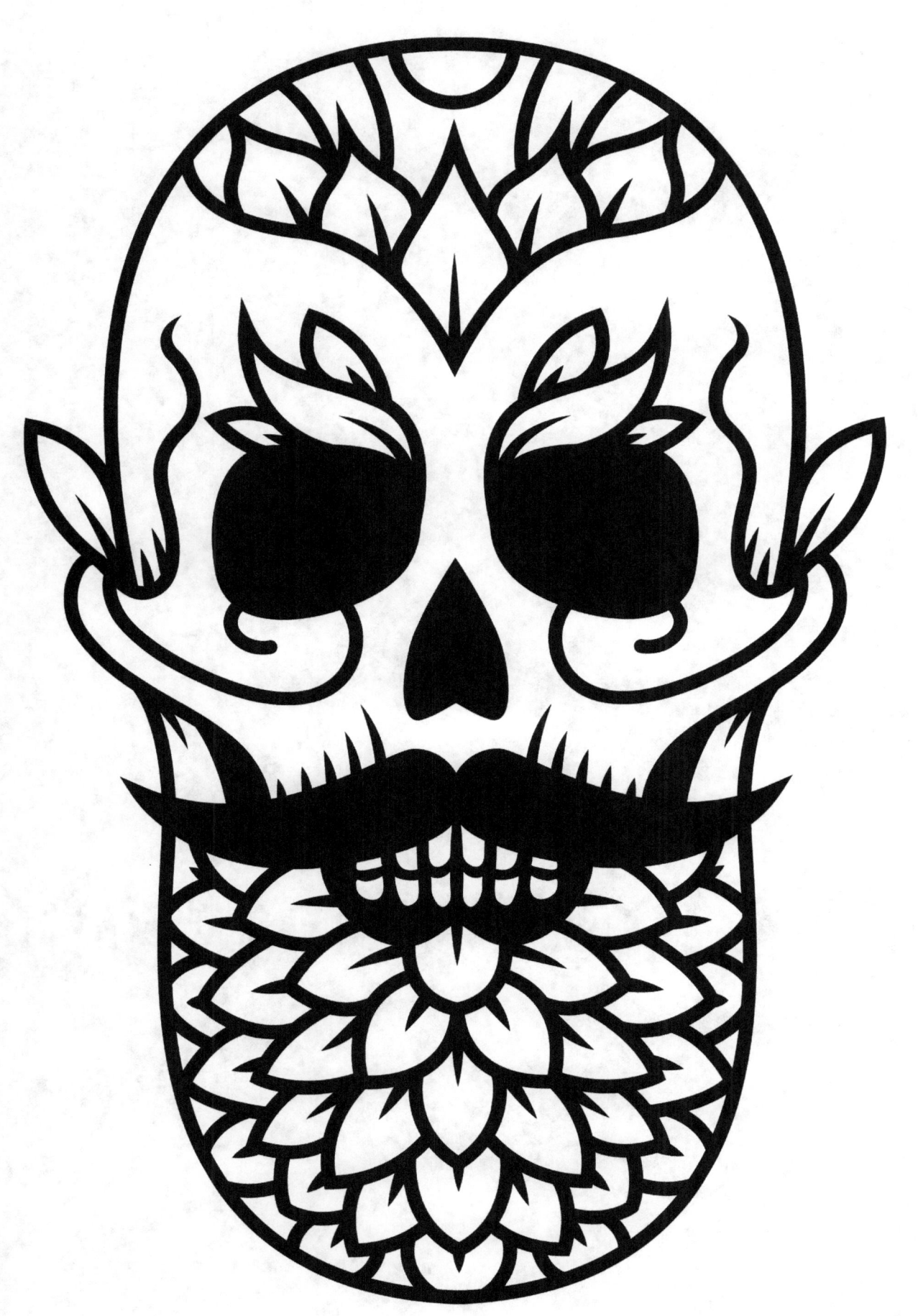

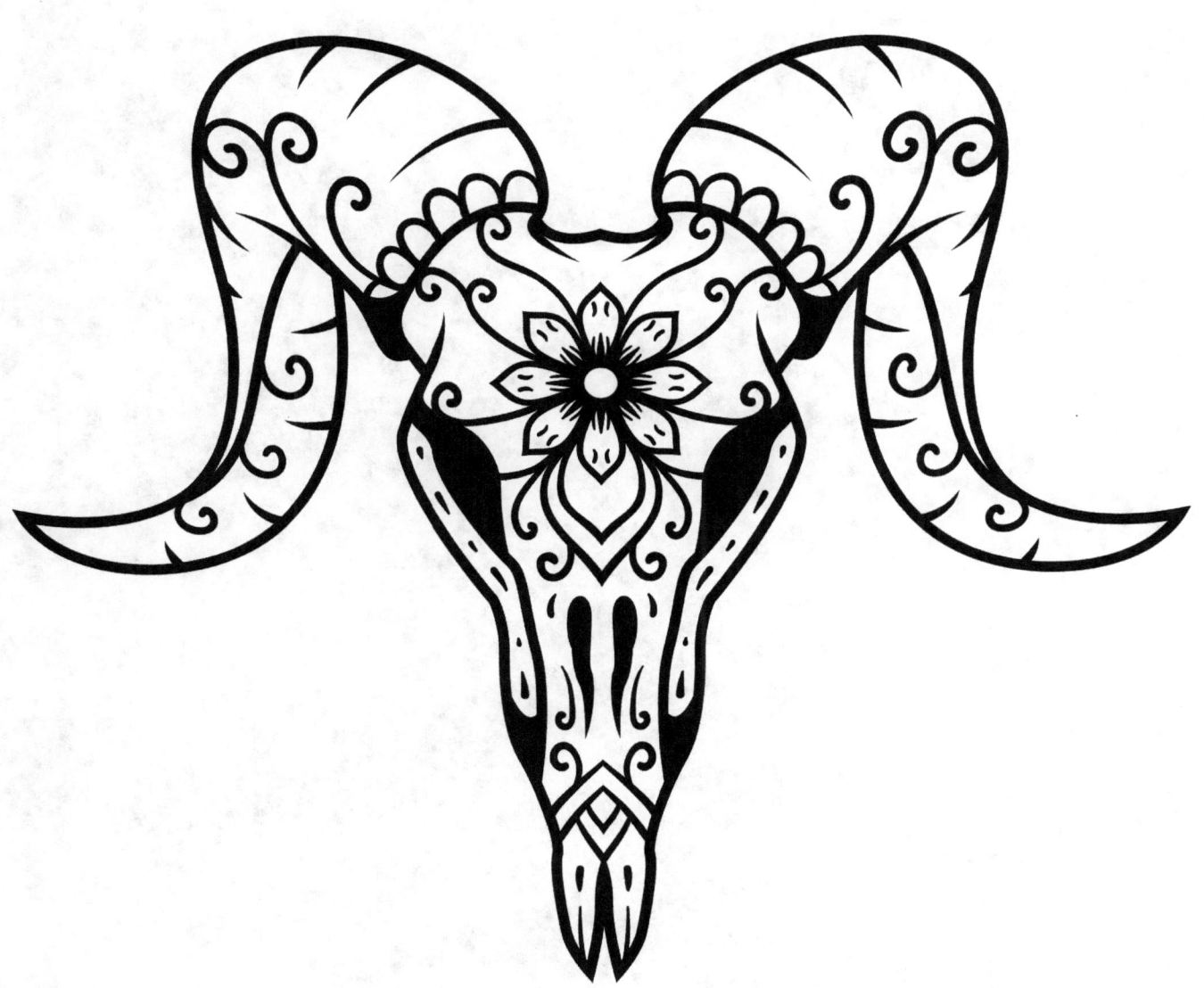

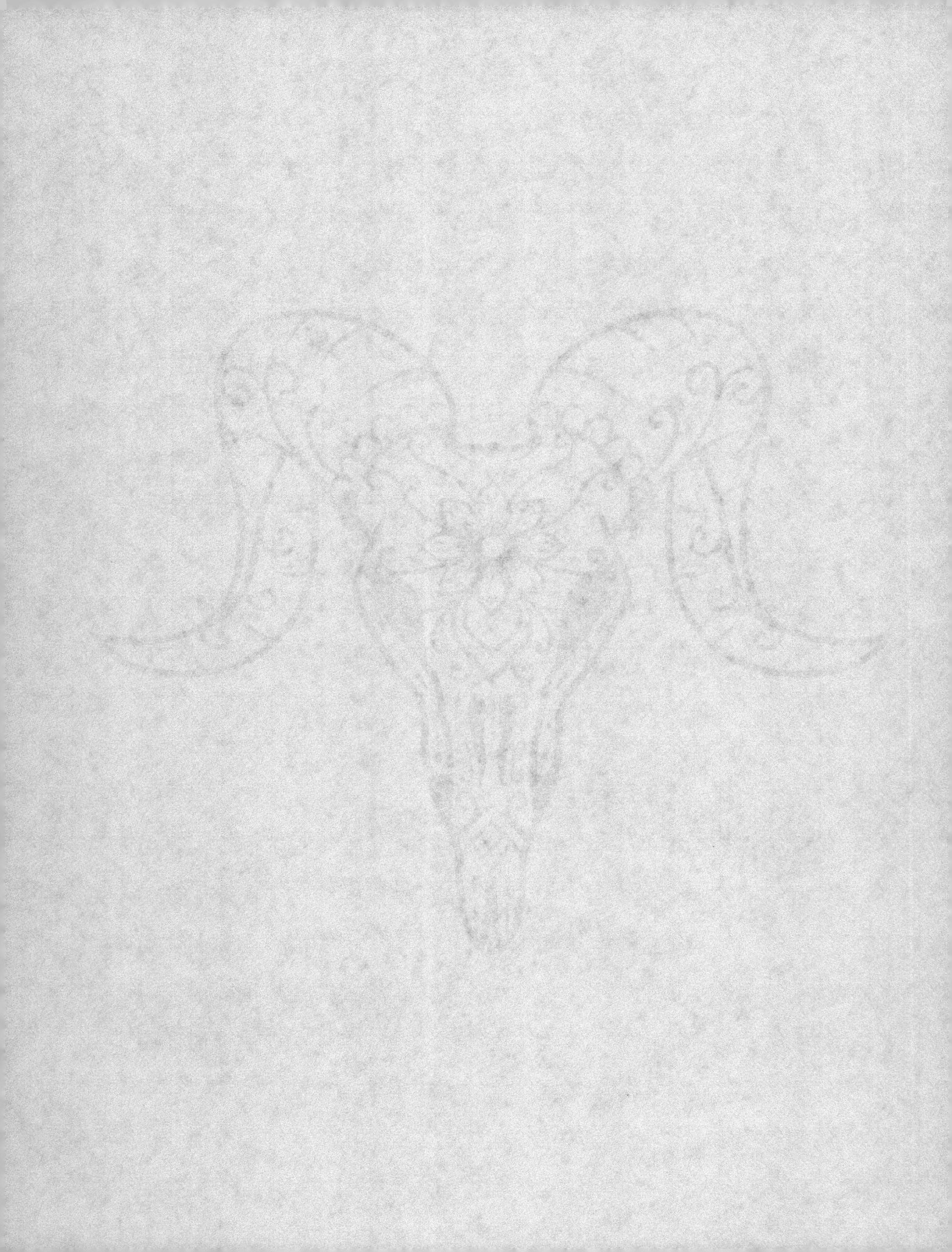

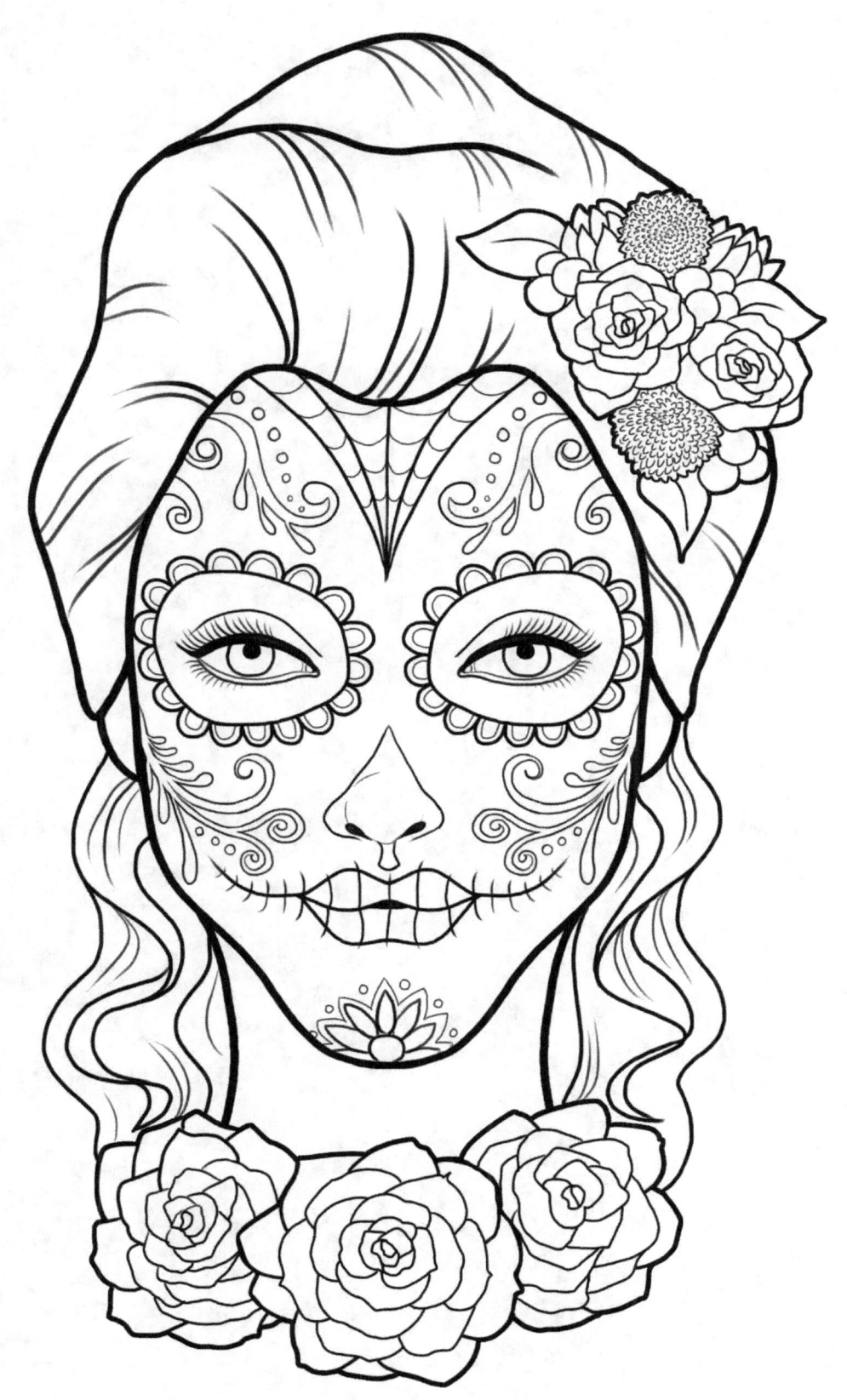

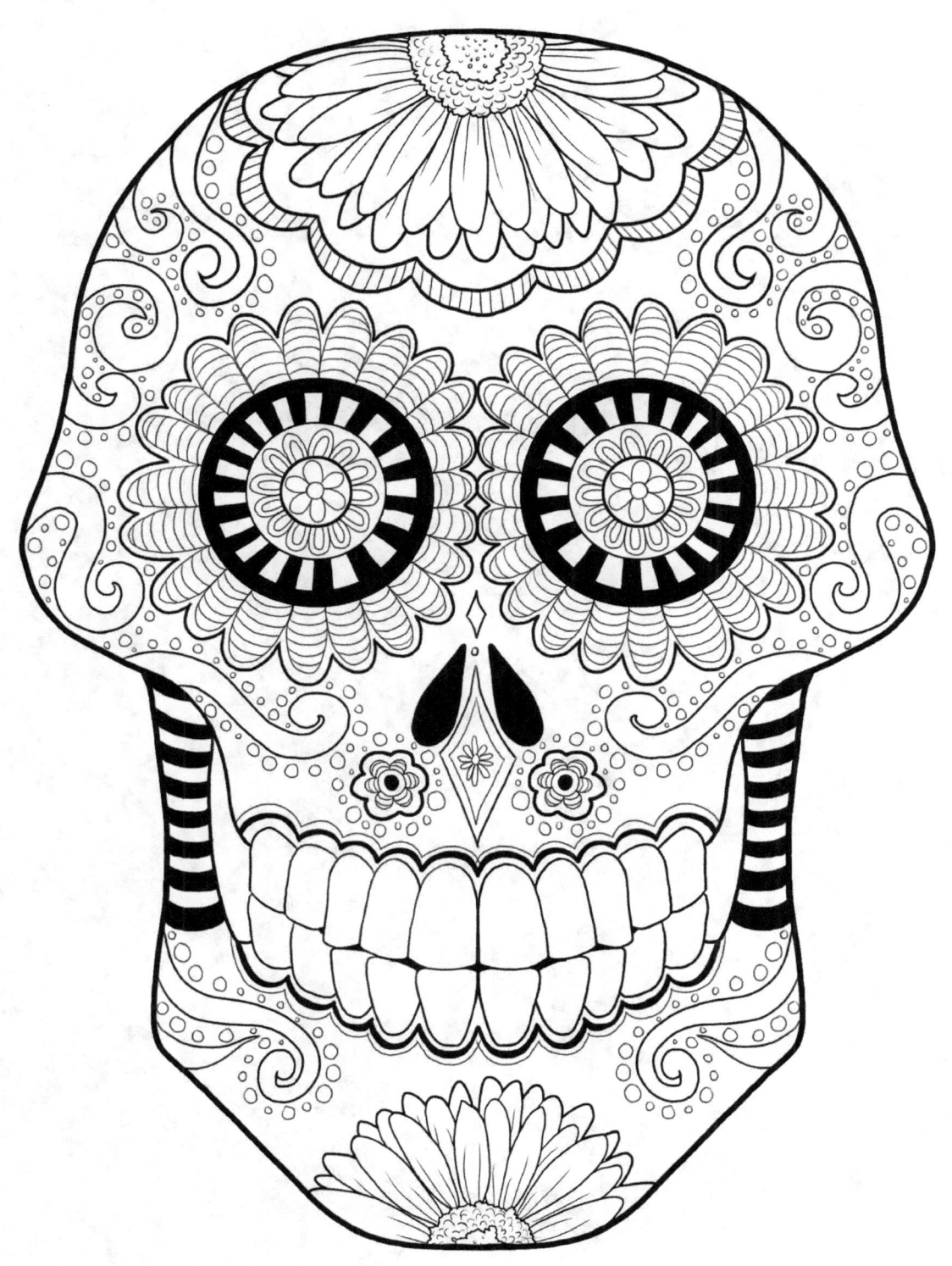

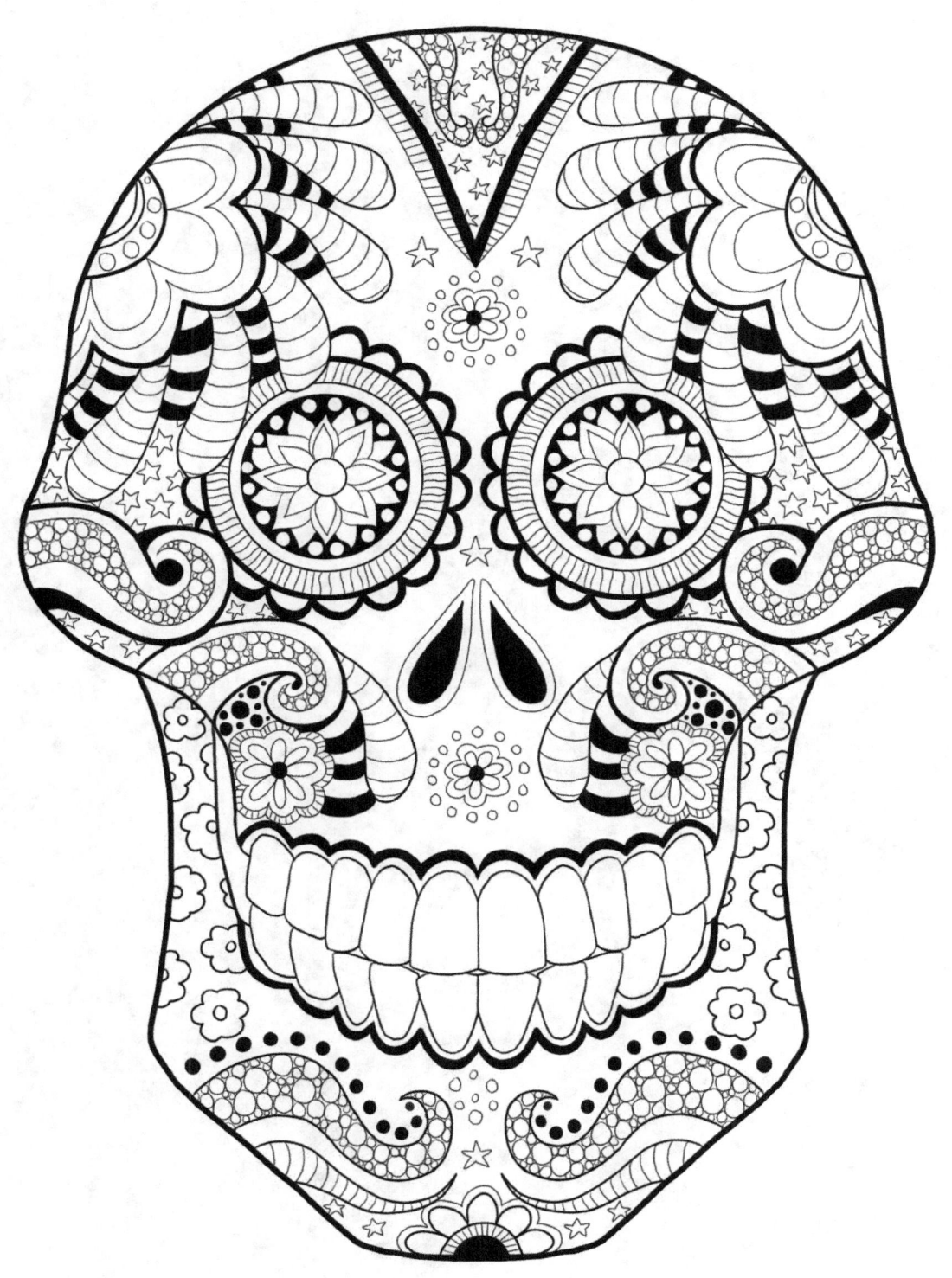

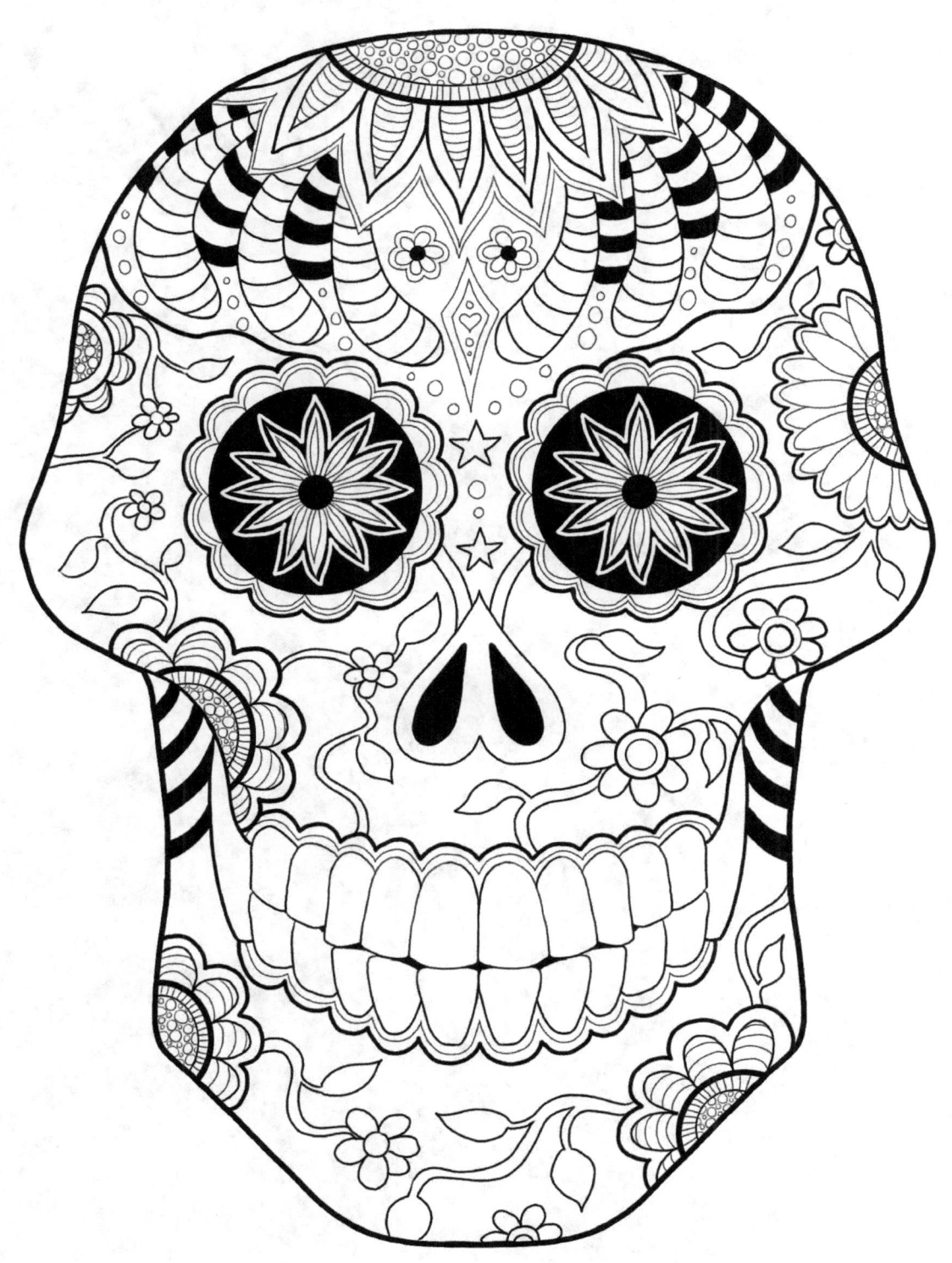

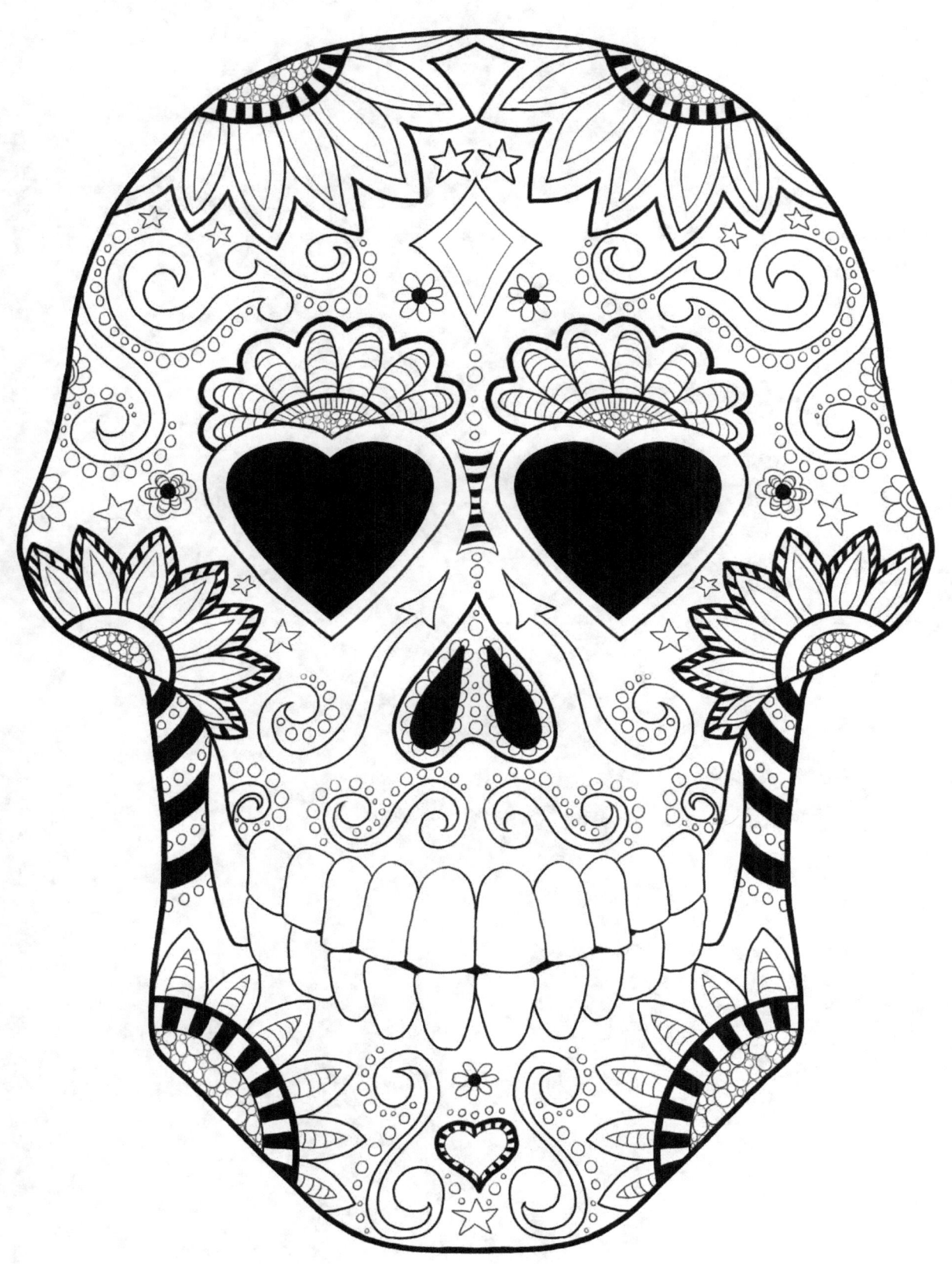

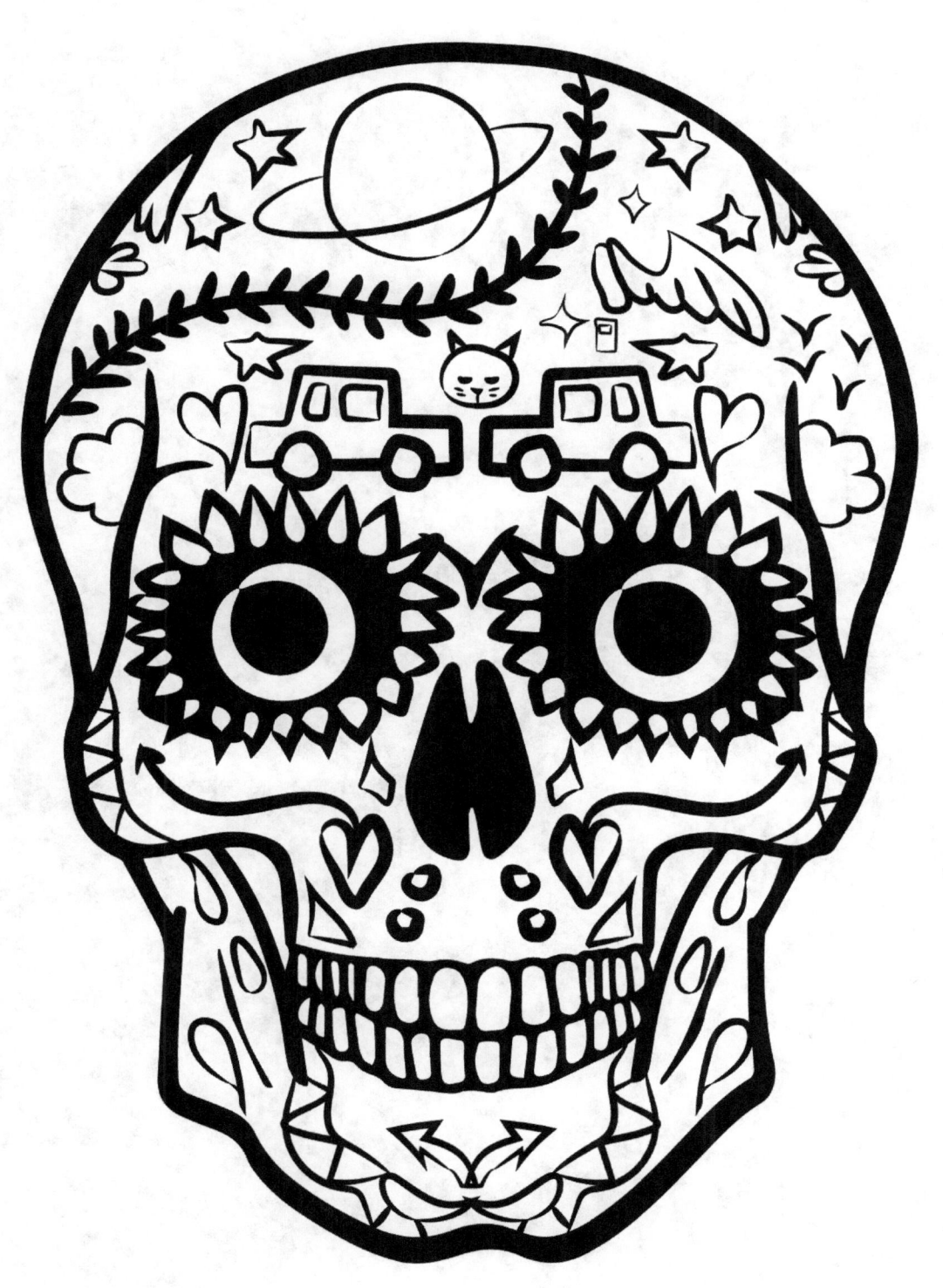

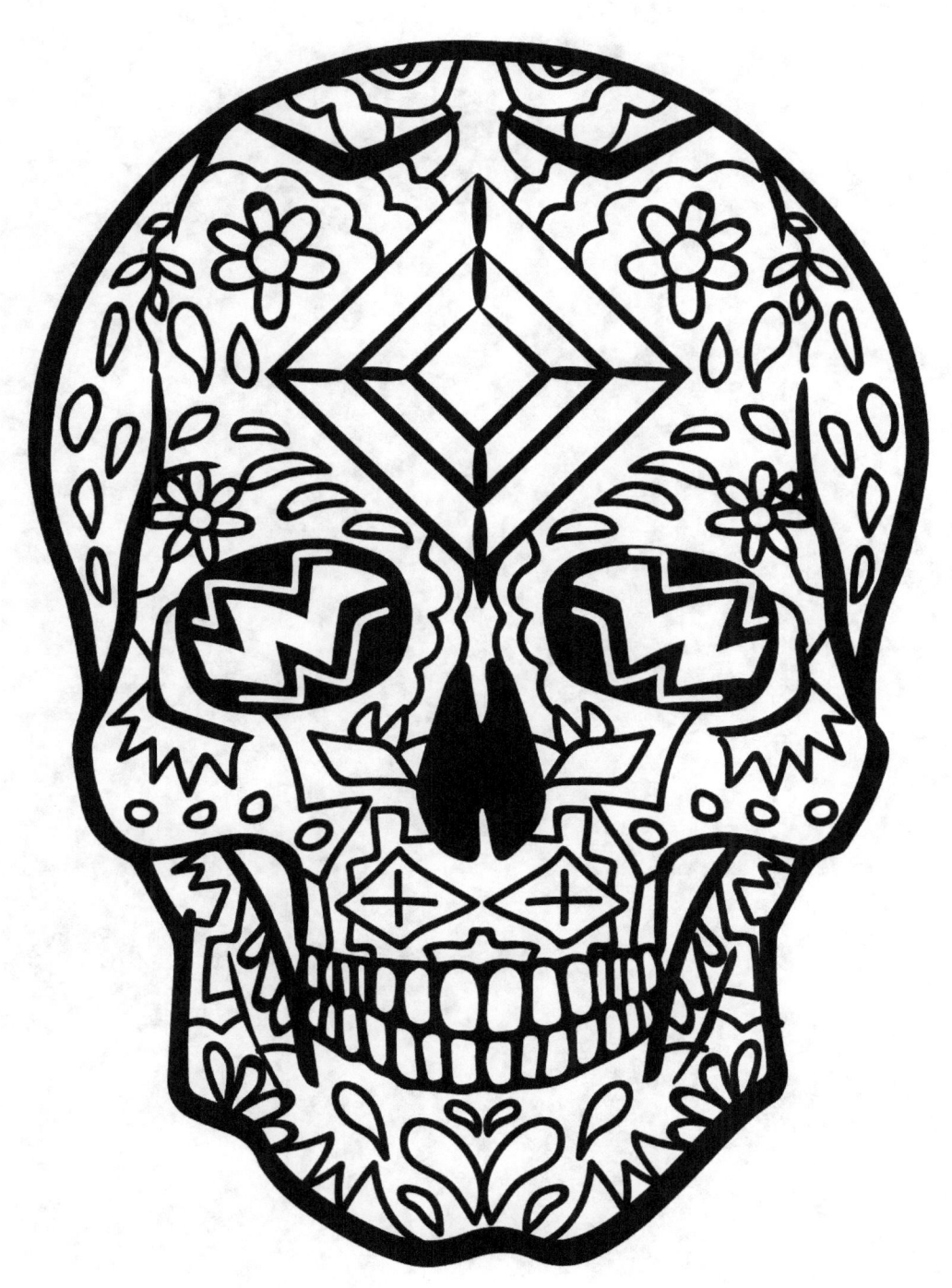

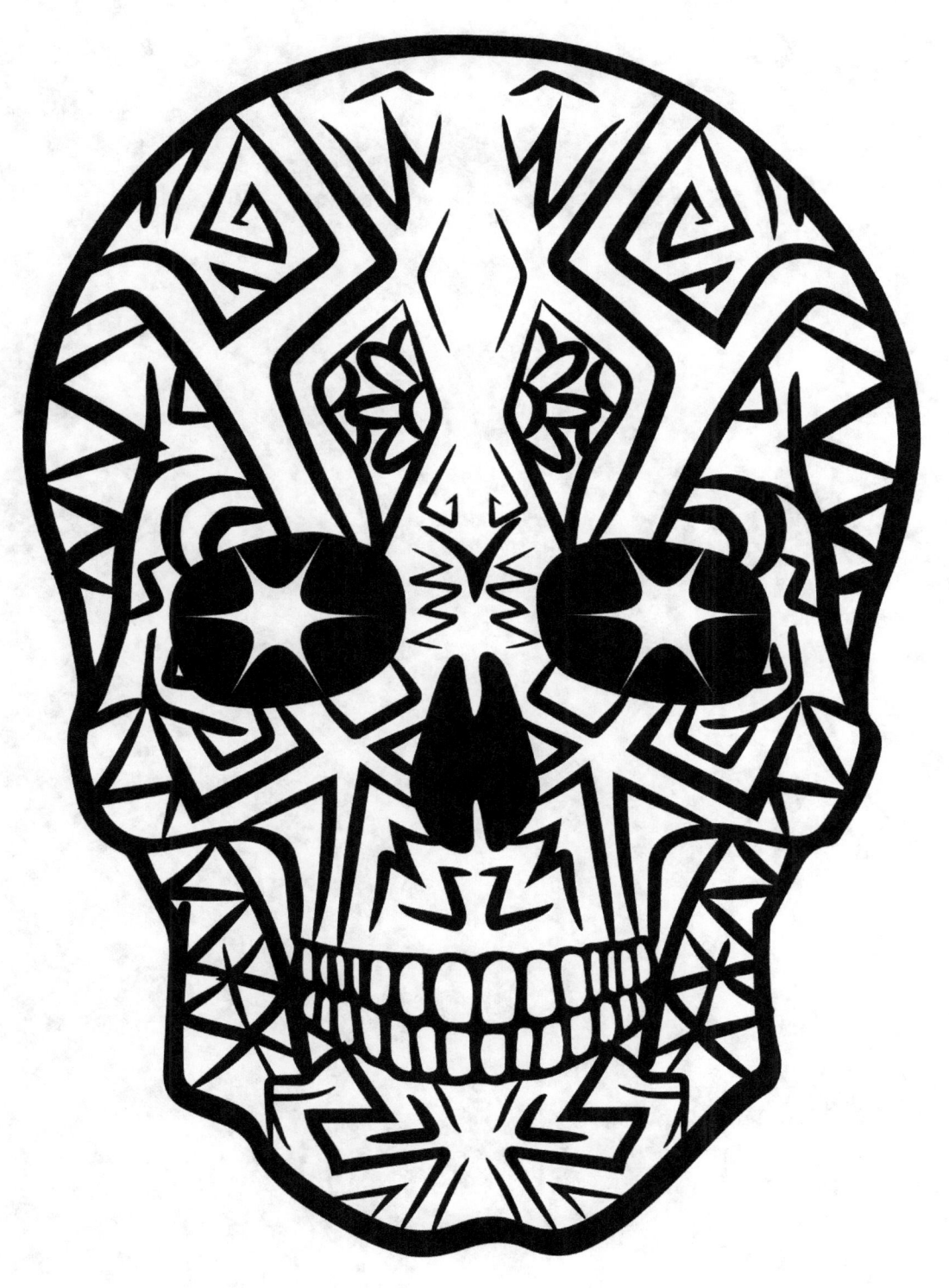

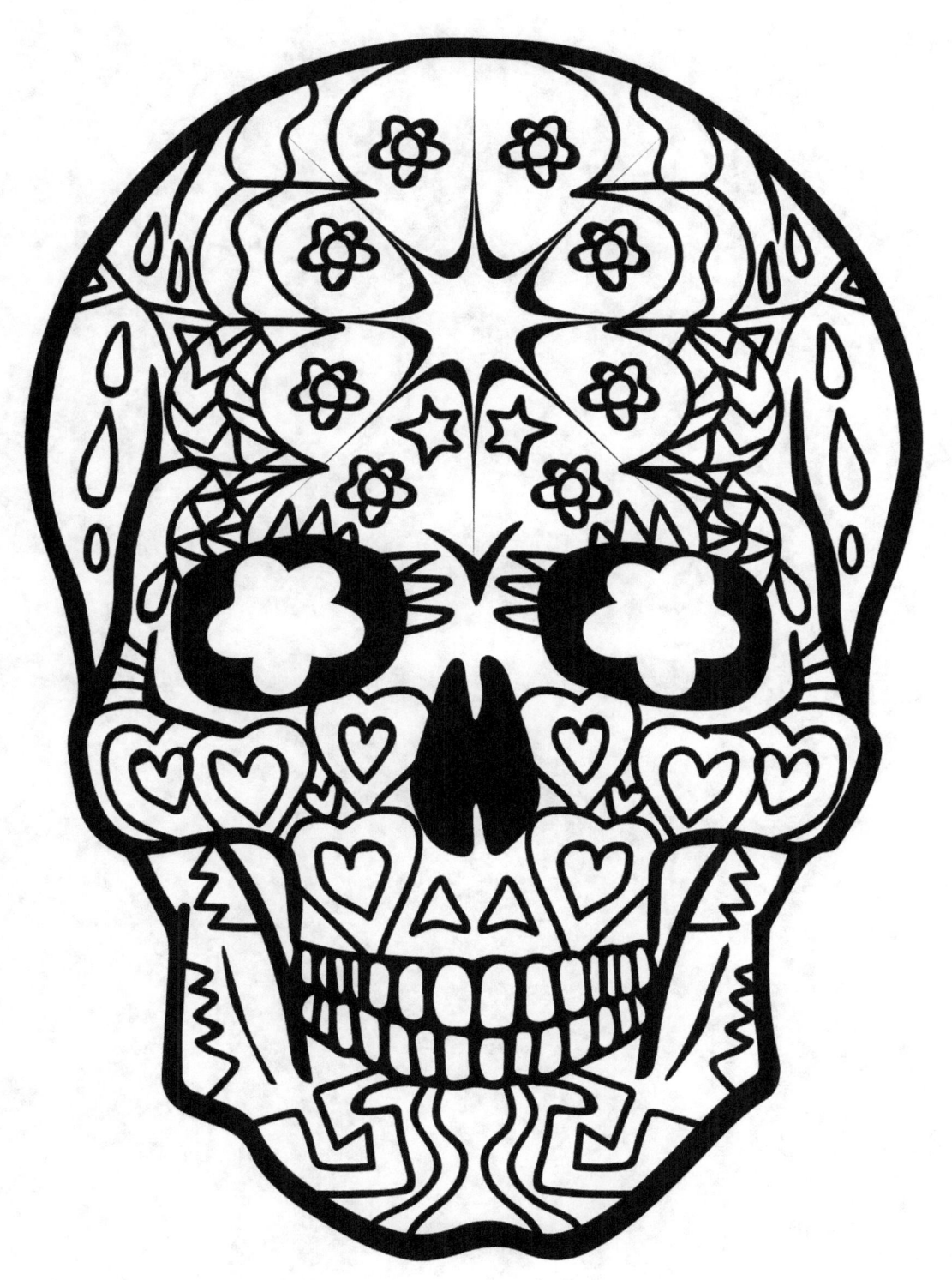

www.ingramcontent.com/pod-product-compliance
Lightning Source LLC
Chambersburg PA
CBHW060441220526
45465CB00008B/3223